A CHARGE KEPT

D1124913

THE RECORD

OF THE

BUSH PRESIDENCY

2001–2009

Edited by Marc A. Thiessen

CONTENTS

INTRODUCTION

"We have served America through one of the most consequential periods of our history."

– President George W. Bush

On January 20, 2001, President George W. Bush and Vice President Richard B. Cheney were sworn into office. They brought with them a clear philosophy and a set of policies to make America stronger, more competitive, and more hopeful. They promised to:

- Rebuild and transform our Armed Forces and our alliances to meet the threats of the 21st century.

- Raise standards in education and bring accountability to public schools so that no child in America is left behind.

- Reduce taxes and unleash the entrepreneurial spirit of our citizens.

- Strengthen America's "armies of compassion" by supporting faith-based and community groups.

- Provide unprecedented support for America's veterans.

- Resist the twin temptations of isolationism and protectionism by engaging the world with confidence and promoting free trade.

- Harness America's innovative spirit to develop new energy technologies, reduce our dependence on foreign oil, and preserve the beauty and quality of our environment.

- Reform our health care system, and make health care more affordable and more accessible for more Americans.

- Foster a culture of life and affirm in law the dignity of every human life.

- Appoint judges who respect our Constitution and laws, and do not legislate from the bench.

- Take on seemingly intractable challenges such as reforming our immigration system and Social Security.

Over the past eight years, President Bush and his Administration worked to meet these pledges. President Bush also adapted to unexpected crises. The greatest of these was the terrorist attacks that killed nearly 3,000 people on September 11, 2001. President Bush responded with a bold strategy to protect the American people. He reorganized the government and strengthened our defenses at home. He rallied allies to confront terrorists and their state sponsors abroad. And he launched a historic effort to support freedom and democracy as an alternative to tyranny and terror, especially in the Middle East.

Many of the President's efforts were successful. Some were not. History will record, however, that the 43rd President confronted tough problems, so as not to pass them on to future generations. He did not base his decisions on popularity or opinion polls. His charge was to uphold the honor and dignity of the office entrusted to him by the American people and leave America a better and safer Nation. And that is a charge he kept.

KEEPING AMERICA SAFE

For many Americans, the war on terror began on September 11, 2001. But the threat to our Nation emerged long before. Throughout the 1980s and 1990s, the followers of a hateful and radical ideology grew in strength and ambition. These extremists unleashed an unprecedented campaign of terror against the United States. In 1993, they attacked the World Trade Center. In 1998, they bombed two of our embassies in Africa. And in 2000, they struck the USS Cole.

Then came September 11, 2001. In the space of a single morning, 19 terrorists claimed nearly 3,000 lives. By nightfall, the sun had set on a very different world. With rumors of more attacks swirling, Americans went to bed wondering what the future would bring.

On that night, few people could have imagined that more than seven years would pass without another terrorist attack on American soil. This is not for lack of effort on the part of the terrorists. Working with allies around the world, the United States has stopped several al Qaeda attacks on our homeland. These attacks include a 2002 plot to fly a plane into the tallest building in Los Angeles, a 2003 plot to crash airplanes into targets on the East Coast, and a 2006 plot to blow up multiple passenger jets flying across the Atlantic from Britain to North America.

The success we have had in keeping America safe is a tribute to the men and women who have toiled day and night to defend this land. It is also a testament to the wise and farsighted decisions that President Bush made beginning immediately after 9/11.

President Bush responded to the attacks by launching a broad and sustained war on terrorist networks across the globe. He promised the American people: "[W]e will direct every resource at our command to win the war against terrorists: every means of diplomacy, every tool of intelligence, every instrument of law enforcement, every financial influence. We will starve the terrorists of funding, turn them against each other, rout them out of their safe hiding places and bring them to justice."

The President has followed through on this commitment. Under the President's leadership, the United States has bolstered its homeland security and intelligence capabilities, taken the fight to the terrorists abroad, and countered their ideology of death and destruction with an alternative vision of freedom and hope. And as President Bush departs from office, he leaves behind the policies, alliances, and institutions needed to prevail in the long struggle ahead.

The Bush Doctrine

In this new war, President Bush set forth a doctrine with three key elements:

First, the United States would make no distinction between those who commit acts of terror and those who support and harbor them.

Second, America would not wait to be attacked again. We would confront grave threats before they fully materialize. We would stay on the offense against the terrorists – fighting them abroad so we did not have to face them here at home.

Third, America would counter the hateful ideology of the terrorists by promoting the hopeful alternative of human freedom. The desire for liberty is universal, and in the long run the only path to lasting peace is the advance of freedom in the broader Middle East and across the globe.

The Liberation of Afghanistan

The Bush Doctrine was applied in Afghanistan, immediately after 9/11. The President told the leaders of the Taliban regime that they must close every terrorist training camp and hand over every terrorist to appropriate authorities. He told them they must give the United States full access to the terrorist training camps so we could ensure they were no longer operating. And he told them these demands were not up for negotiation. He gave the Taliban a choice: comply immediately or share the same fate as the terrorists.

The Taliban regime refused to comply with these just demands. So on October 7, 2001, the United States and its coalition partners launched Operation Enduring Freedom. This operation removed the Taliban from power, captured or killed hundreds of Taliban and al Qaeda fighters, shut down the terrorist camps where the enemy planned 9/11, and liberated 25 million Afghans.

The Hunt for Al Qaeda

After the fall of the Taliban, the Administration remained on the offensive and kept the pressure on the terrorists. Since 9/11, America and its allies have captured or killed hundreds of al Qaeda leaders, managers, and operatives.

Those brought to justice include many of al Qaeda's operational commanders – the senior leaders responsible for day-to-day planning of terrorist activities across the globe.

Today, because America has stayed on the offensive, al Qaeda has been weakened, and many of those responsible for the destruction of 9/11 are in custody in Guantanamo Bay, Cuba, awaiting trial.

While Osama bin Laden and Ayman Zawahiri remain at large at the time of this writing, they are in hiding, under pressure, and unable to direct the day-to-day operations of the al Qaeda network as they once did.

The Removal of Saddam Hussein

Saddam Hussein was a dictator who had pursued and used weapons of mass destruction, sponsored terrorists, paid the families of suicide bombers, invaded his neighbors, brutalized his people, deceived international inspectors, and refused to comply with more than a dozen United Nations (UN) resolutions. In 2003, when the UN Security Council gave him one final chance to disclose and disarm or face serious consequences, he refused. Saddam Hussein had a clear choice between peaceful disclosure or war – and he chose war. President Bush assembled an international coalition. And on March 19, 2003, coalition forces crossed into Iraq to remove Saddam Hussein and his Ba'athist regime from power.

The overthrow of Saddam Hussein's regime liberated 25 million Iraqis. And it had benefits beyond Iraq's borders. The leader of Libya announced in December 2003 that he was abandoning his country's pursuit of weapons of mass destruction. The Libyan nuclear program – the uranium, the centrifuges, the designs to build bombs, as well as key missile components – was flown to secure storage facilities in the United States. Libya committed to destroy its chemical weapons. Today, Libya is out of the business of pursuing weapons of mass destruction and off the list of state sponsors of terror.

Public disclosure of Libya's weapons of mass destruction programs gave momentum to international efforts to roll up the A.Q. Khan nuclear proliferation network, which had spread sensitive nuclear technology to Libya, Iran, and North Korea. Today, A.Q. Khan's activities have been restricted, and his international network for disseminating nuclear technology has been largely dismantled.

In the years that followed the overthrow of Saddam Hussein, there was difficult fighting in Iraq. Our men and women in uniform have made enormous sacrifices in Iraq, and more than 4,200 have given their lives. As the President stated, "[t]he battle in Iraq has been longer and harder and more costly than we anticipated." But he also reminded the American people that "after September the 11th, America decided that we would fight the war on terror on the offense, and that we would confront threats before they fully materialized. Saddam Hussein was a threat to the United States of America. America is safer today because Saddam Hussein is no longer in power."

New Alliances

To prevail in the war on terror, President Bush built new alliances to confront the threats of a new century. He formed a coalition of more than 90 nations to fight the war on terror. These nations are working together in many different ways. Some are sharing intelligence. Some are freezing terrorist assets or breaking up terrorist cells on their territory. Some are providing airlift, basing, over-flight, and refueling. Others are contributing air, sea, and ground forces, combat air patrols, mine clearing, and special operations forces. Some are helping to confront the ideology of the enemy. Some are helping quietly, others openly. Each is making important contributions to the war on terror.

The President's diplomacy and leadership encouraged nations like Saudi Arabia to launch crackdowns on al Qaeda and its allies. Indonesia crippled the terrorist group Jemaah Islamiyah, which had worked with al Qaeda in planning attacks against the American homeland. The Philippines worked to combat the Abu Sayyaf terrorist group, an al Qaeda affiliate. Algerian forces have struck blows against al Qaeda's North Africa wing. In Europe, security services have broken up al Qaeda and al Qaeda-related or inspired cells in Germany, Denmark, Turkey, the United Kingdom, Italy, France, the Netherlands, and Belgium.

In Iraq, more than 140,000 troops from 41 other nations have served as part of the coalition. Forces from all these countries have served bravely, and many made the ultimate sacrifice.

The President assembled a broad coalition in Afghanistan. And in 2003, NATO took over the International Security Assistance Force in that country. This NATO mission increased from a small force operating only in the capital city of Kabul to a large multinational force that is leading operations across all of Afghanistan. At the end of 2008, approximately 62,000 personnel from all 26 NATO countries and 17 partner nations were serving in Afghanistan, helping the Afghan people defend their freedom and rebuild their country. Afghanistan is the most difficult and ambitious mission NATO has ever taken on – and the first mission in the history of the Alliance outside the North Atlantic Area.

New Institutions, Authorities, and Programs

As the Bush Administration mobilized the international community to meet the terrorist threat, it also built institutions, obtained authorities, and established programs necessary to protect America.

The Bush Administration undertook the most sweeping reorganization of the Federal Government in half a century. Not since President Truman worked with Congress to create the Department of Defense, the National Security Council, the CIA, and other institutions to fight the Cold War, has an American President done more to transform the national security institutions of this country. Working with Congress, the President created the new Department of Homeland Security – merging 22 different government organizations into a single department with a clear mission: to secure the homeland and protect America from future attacks.

At the Department of Defense, the President created: a new Northern Command responsible for homeland defense; a new Africa Command to help America's friends and allies on that continent promote stability and protect against transnational threats; a transformed U.S. Special Operations Command – more than doubling its budget, adding thousands of new troops, and making it the lead command in the global war on terror; and a retooled U.S. Strategic Command, with responsibility for combating weapons of mass destruction.

President Bush launched the largest transformation of the Army in over a century. He helped lead the most dramatic transformation of the NATO Alliance since its founding in 1949 – bringing in seven new members, creating a new NATO Response Force, and deploying NATO forces outside Europe for the first time in the history of the Alliance.

The President also:

- Signed a new law establishing the position of Director of National Intelligence and directed a broad restructuring of our Nation's intelligence agencies to address the threats of the 21st century.

- Created the National Counterterrorism Center, where personnel from Federal, State, and local departments and agencies work side by side to track terrorist threat reporting and prevent new attacks.

- Reorganized the Department of Justice and the FBI to focus on preventing terrorism.

- Created a new Office of Terrorism and Financial Intelligence at the Department of the Treasury, tasked with tracking the finances of terrorists, proliferators, and rogue states and denying the enemy the funds they need to threaten our country.

- Worked with Congress to enact the USA PATRIOT Act – breaking down barriers that had prevented America's law enforcement and intelligence agencies from sharing vital information on terrorist threats.

- Secured Congressional approval of legislation allowing our intelligence community to effectively monitor foreign terrorist communications – to help us learn who the terrorists are talking to and what they are planning.

- Secured Congressional approval of the Military Commissions Act – so that captured terrorists accused of war crimes can be brought to justice for their acts.

- Authorized a program at the Central Intelligence Agency to detain and question key terrorist leaders and operatives – so we can find out what captured terrorists know about planned attacks. Were it not for this program, our intelligence community believes that al Qaeda and its allies would have succeeded in launching another attack against the American homeland.

New Measures to Protect the Homeland

As he reformed government to help prevent terrorist attacks, President Bush provided unprecedented funding and support for our law enforcement, intelligence, and homeland security communities.

To stop terrorists from infiltrating our country, the President made our borders more secure and deployed new technologies for screening people entering America. The Administration:

- Doubled the number of Border Patrol agents to more than 18,000, and increased their funding by more than 60 percent.

- Unified the Federal Government's various watchlisting databases into one central database and created a program to screen visiting foreign nationals using biometrics and other advanced technologies.

- Improved the way we evaluate visa applicants and made it harder to counterfeit travel documents.

- Ramped up enforcement of our Nation's immigration laws in the interior of the United States, including at the country's worksites.

The President increased the number of Federal marshals on passenger flights. He also created the new Transportation Security Administration to screen commercial air passengers in the country.

To stop terrorists from smuggling biological, chemical, and nuclear weapons into American cities, the Administration deployed a layered system of protections that starts overseas, continues along our borders, and extends throughout our country. Today, we partner with the world's leading U.S. importers to pre-screen cargo entering the country and examine high-risk maritime cargo at foreign seaports before they are loaded on vessels destined for the United States. In addition, the people who load and unload cargo are properly credentialed. The Administration also launched programs to protect major metropolitan areas by providing early detection of biological, nuclear, or radiological attacks. For example, a groundbreaking air monitoring system that can detect biological agents and sound a lifesaving warning now operates in 30 U.S. cities.

To protect our critical infrastructure from terrorist attacks, the Administration worked with the private sector to develop security plans for 18 of the Nation's key sectors – including our food and water supplies, nuclear and chemical facilities, power grids, and telecommunications networks. Under Operation Neptune Shield, the men and women of the Coast Guard are protecting more than 360 ports and more than 95,000 miles of coastline. The Administration took actions to protect our transportation systems, including new steps to protect airports, railways, and mass transit systems.

To better defend against cyber attacks, the Administration launched the Comprehensive National Cybersecurity Initiative and created a new National Cyber Security Division at the Department of Homeland Security charged with protecting against virtual terrorism.

To improve our capacity to prevent and, if necessary, respond to terrorist attacks, the President strengthened Federal cooperation with State and local governments. Today, there are 21st century lines of communication in place that allow Federal officials to share classified threat information rapidly and securely. The Administration also helped State and local officials establish intelligence fusion centers in 48 States. These centers allow Federal officials to provide intelligence to their State and local partners and allow locally-generated information to get to officials who need it in Washington.

Since September 2001, the Bush Administration has provided cities and States with more than $27 billion in homeland security grants; worked with officials in 75 major metropolitan areas to improve the ability of first responders to communicate clearly in an emergency; supported mutual aid agreements among States; and strengthened the Emergency Management Assistance Compact – so that when communities need help from their neighbors, the right assistance will get to the right people at the right time.

The Nation's stockpile of drugs and vaccines that would be needed in the event of a bioterrorist attack or a mass casualty incident has been expanded. The Federal Government now has enough smallpox vaccine for every American. The Administration also increased our investments in bio-defense medical research and development at the National Institutes of Health by more than 3,000 percent – from $53 million in 2001 to more than $1.7 billion today. The Administration also launched Project BioShield – an effort to speed the development of new vaccines and treatments against chemical, biological, radiological, and nuclear agents that could be used in a terrorist attack.

In total, the Bush Administration nearly tripled funding for homeland security since 2001. This has made America safer, but we are not yet safe. As the President put it, in a free society "there's no such thing as perfect security. . . . To attack us, the terrorists only have to be right once – to stop them, we need to be right 100 percent of the time." Over the past eight years, the Administration worked to stop new attacks – and to ensure that if an attack does occur, America will be ready.

The Freedom Agenda and the War on Terror

The President believes that, in the long run, the best way to protect the homeland is to defeat the hateful ideology of the terrorists – by spreading the hopeful alternative of human freedom. From the beginning, the President understood that the war on terror is an ideological struggle. He saw how dictatorships in the Middle East fed resentment and despair, and how extremists exploit the hopelessness caused by hunger, poverty, disease, and a lack of freedom to recruit terrorists and suicide bombers for attacks against free nations.

The President put it this way: "On September the 11th, 2001, we saw that problems originating in a failed and oppressive state 7,000 miles away could bring murder and destruction to our country. And we learned an important lesson: Decades of excusing and accommodating the lack of freedom in the Middle East did nothing to make us safe. So long as the Middle East remains a place where freedom does not flourish, it will remain a place where terrorists foment resentment and threaten American security."

The President's belief that freedom could flourish in the Middle East draws inspiration from examples in history. The rise of young democracies in Germany and Japan helped yield peace in Europe and Asia – regions once racked by conflict and war. Convinced a similar transformation was possible in the broader Middle East, President Bush launched what he called "a forward strategy for freedom." This strategy was based on a clear premise: "The desire for freedom is universal, written by the Almighty into the hearts of every man, woman, and child on this Earth.... [W]e know that when free societies take root in that part of the world, they will yield the peace we all desire.... And by bringing freedom to these societies, we replace hatred with hope, and this will help us to marginalize the extremists, and eliminate the conditions that feed radicalism, and make the American people more secure."

During his eight years in office, the President stood with democrats and reformers across the region – and time and again, his confidence in the universality of freedom was vindicated. Millions of Muslims in the broader Middle East courageously stepped forward to claim their liberty and embrace the cause of democracy and self-government. In Afghanistan, 8 million people defied terrorist threats and went to the polls to choose their leaders. In Iraq, nearly 12 million people refused to let the car bombers and assassins stop them from voting for the free future of their country. In Lebanon, more than a million people voted for a free and sovereign government to rule their land. In Pakistan, 35 million people cast their ballots in that country's recent election. Over time, the examples set by these young democracies will inspire more people across the region to claim their liberty as well.

The Surge in Iraq

A battle between freedom and terror unfolded in Iraq. When Saddam Hussein's regime was removed in 2003, former regime elements took off their uniforms and blended into the countryside to fight the emergence of a free Iraq. They were joined by foreign terrorists seeking to establish safe havens from which to plot new attacks.

Despite attacks by terrorists and insurgents, sovereignty was transferred to the Iraqis in 2004; millions of Iraqis voted in the January 2005 elections to elect an interim government; the Iraqis drafted the most progressive and democratic constitution in the Arab world; Iraqis went to the polls in October 2005 to approve that constitution; and millions of Iraqis voted in the December 2005 elections to form a permanent government under that constitution.

While the terrorists failed to stop these steps on the road to democracy, they made other advances. They succeeded in establishing safe havens in many parts of the country. They succeeded in killing and terrorizing Iraqi civilians, and intimidating those who opposed their grim ideology. They succeeded in creating sectarian divisions among Iraqis – pitting Iraqis against each other in an effort to sow chaos.

In February of 2006, the terrorists blew up one of Shia Islam's holiest shrines, the Golden Mosque in Samarra. This atrocity was designed to provoke retaliation from the Iraqi Shia, and it worked. Radical Shia elements, many with support from Iran, formed death squads and launched retaliatory attacks. The result was a tragic escalation of sectarian rage and reprisals. Over the course of 2006, Iraq's young democracy was increasingly in peril – as chaos spread, the terrorists seized new ground, and the nation neared the point of political collapse and civil war.

The President understood that America could not retreat in the face of terror. He knew that if America did not act, the violence that had been consuming Iraq could worsen, spread, and eventually reach genocidal levels. Baghdad could have disintegrated into a contagion of killing, and Iraq could have descended into full-blown sectarian warfare. The chaos in Iraq could have spread across the region, emboldened Iran, emboldened the terrorists, and given them a new base from which to launch operations against America and its allies.

In response to the deteriorating situation in Iraq, President Bush decided to send additional forces into the country focused on population security in a policy shift that became known as "the surge." He gave our troops a new commander, General David Petraeus. And he gave our troops a new mission: Work with Iraqi forces to protect the Iraqi people, pursue the enemy in its strongholds, and deny the terrorists sanctuary anywhere in the country.

With the help of the reinforcements the President sent, our troops took advantage of several significant developments in Iraq that preceded the surge:

Between 2003 and 2006, Coalition and Iraqi forces had made progress in dismantling terrorist networks; the Iraqi Security Forces had grown in number and effectiveness; and the Iraqis had stood up a democratic government, led by Prime Minister Maliki.

In addition, in the fall of 2006, Sunni tribal leaders in Anbar province grew tired of al Qaeda's brutality and started a popular uprising called the "Anbar Awakening." These tribal leaders sought America's help in the fight against al Qaeda. To take advantage of this opportunity, the President sent 4,000 Marines to Anbar as part of the surge. Together, American troops, Iraqi forces, and the Sunni tribes drove al Qaeda from strongholds in Anbar and took the province back for the Iraqi people. Over the course of 2007, similar movements spread across the country, as Iraqis stepped forward to take up arms against the terrorists and extremists. These movements grew into a grassroots surge that eventually included more than 100,000 Iraqi citizens. The government in Baghdad stepped forward with a surge of its own, adding more than 100,000 new Iraqi soldiers and police by 2007.

Over time, as Iraqi forces became more capable, security operations became increasingly Iraqi-led, with American forces playing a supporting role. For example, in early 2008, the Iraqi Government launched successful military operations against Shia extremist groups in places

13

like Basra, al-Amarah, and Baghdad. And later that year, Iraqi forces led operations against al Qaeda in and around the northern city of Mosul and in Diyala Province.

As a result of these efforts, the situation in Iraq has been transformed. Violence is down dramatically, as are coalition and Iraq Security Force casualties, improvised explosive device attacks, and suicide attacks. Normal life has returned to communities across the country. Political reconciliation is moving forward, and the Iraqi government has passed budgets and major pieces of legislation, including a provincial elections law, a provincial powers law, a pension law, and a de-Ba'athification reform law.

The surge did more than turn around the situation in Iraq – it made possible a major strategic victory in the broader war on terror. For the terrorists, Iraq was supposed to be the place where al Qaeda rallied Iraqis to drive America out. Instead, Iraq became the place where the Iraqis joined forces with America to drive al Qaeda out. As a result, al Qaeda suffered more than a military defeat in Iraq – it suffered an ideological defeat as well. Across the region, people saw that al Qaeda in Iraq could be vanquished, and that a future of terror was not foreordained.

The surge also made it possible for the President to begin bringing our troops home under a policy he called "Return on Success." These troop withdrawals began in late 2007, and by the summer of 2008, the President had brought home all five of the Army combat brigades, the Marine expeditionary unit, and two Marine battalions that were sent to Iraq as part of the surge. In September 2008, he announced additional troop reductions. In a speech at the National Defense University, the President declared: "Over the next several months, we will bring home about 3,400 combat support forces – including aviation personnel, explosive ordnance teams, combat and construction engineers, military police, and logistical support forces. By November, we will bring home a Marine battalion that is now serving in Anbar province. And in February of 2009, another Army combat brigade will come home. This amounts to about 8,000 additional American troops returning home without replacement." In November, with violence in Iraq in dramatic decline, the President approved bringing the Army combat brigade home six weeks early, in time for Christmas.

In December 2008, the Bush Administration concluded two landmark agreements with the Iraqi government – a Strategic Framework Agreement and a Security Agreement (often called a Status of Forces

Agreement). These two agreements formalized the diplomatic, economic, and security ties between the two nations. They build on the success of the surge and the courageous efforts of the Iraqi people to retake their country from the extremists. They cement a strategic partnership between the United States and Iraq. And they pave the way for American forces to return home as the war in Iraq approaches a successful end.

The Strategic Framework Agreement sets out a common vision for U.S.-Iraqi relations in the years ahead. The agreement formalizes "a relationship of friendship and cooperation" between our two countries in the economic, diplomatic, cultural, and security fields. Under this agreement, the United States and Iraq will work together to bring greater stability to Iraq and the region, promote trade and investment, and support Iraq's leaders and their citizens as they strengthen their democratic institutions.

The Security Agreement has provided authority and protection for our soldiers and Defense Department civilians in Iraq since the expiration of the United Nations mandate at the end of 2008. And it lays out a framework for the drawdown of American forces as Iraq becomes increasingly capable of providing for its own security and stability.

With the conclusion of these agreements, President Bush set America's engagement in Iraq on a steady course. He left his successor an Iraq with the enemy in retreat, our forces coming home, and an agreement with Iraqi leaders on the way forward.

None of this would have been possible without the surge and the extraordinary skill, bravery, and sacrifice of our men and women in uniform. Because of them, a door has been opened to a new day in Iraq. And the American people are more secure.

The Quiet Surge in Afghanistan

After September 11, 2001, Coalition forces ousted the Taliban regime, drove al Qaeda from the Afghan sanctuary where they plotted and planned the 9/11 attacks, and helped Afghans begin to build a new democracy. But the enemies of a free Afghanistan refused to give up the fight. They sought to undermine Afghanistan's young democracy so they could regain the dominance they enjoyed in Afghanistan before 9/11. And they ruthlessly attacked innocent Afghans across the country.

In 2006, Afghanistan faced a rise in violence and increasing challenges in establishing effective governance. In response, the Administration undertook a review of U.S. policy and strategy for Afghanistan. Following this review, the Administration launched a "quiet surge" in Afghanistan. The U.S. increased its troop deployments to Afghanistan, including adding a second combat brigade in Regional Command East in early 2007 and 2,400 Marines to Regional Command South in early 2008. At the April 2008 NATO Summit in Bucharest, the President told America's allies that the United States was deploying additional Marines to Afghanistan. Allies increased their force levels as well, with Australia, Bulgaria, the Czech Republic, Denmark, France, Germany, Poland, Slovakia, the United Kingdom, and others sending additional troops to support the NATO mission in Afghanistan. In September 2008, the President announced additional American troop deployments to Afghanistan. In November, a Marine battalion that was scheduled to deploy to Iraq instead deployed to Afghanistan. It was followed in January 2009 by an Army combat brigade. In all, the number of American troops in the country increased from approximately 20,000 two years ago to approximately 31,000 in late 2008. The number of Coalition troops – including NATO troops – increased from approximately 23,000 to approximately 33,000. And the number of trained Afghan army and police forces increased from fewer than 81,000 to 154,000. These troops have a clear mission: to work with Afghan forces to provide security for the Afghan people, protect Afghanistan's infrastructure and democratic institutions, and help ensure access to services like education and health care.

These force increases are making a difference, yet huge challenges in Afghanistan remain. In July 2008, President Bush appointed General David Petraeus as the head of U.S. Central Command – the military command responsible for Iraq, Afghanistan, and the broader Middle East. With this move, the President gave the general who helped turn the battle around in Iraq oversight over our strategy in Afghanistan as well. In November, General Petraeus launched a major review of America's strategy in the entire Central Command area of operations – including Afghanistan. General Petraeus described the challenge in Afghanistan this way: "The effort in Afghanistan is going to be the longest campaign of the long war." In appointing General Petraeus to Central Command, President Bush left our country with an experienced and able commander to help America and its allies prevail.

A Generational Struggle

The President told Congress in his 2007 State of the Union Address: "The war ... we fight today is a generational struggle that will continue long after you and I have turned our duties over to others." But by the actions he took, the institutions he built, the alliances he forged, and the doctrines he set down, President Bush laid the foundation for America's ultimate victory.

⭐

TRANSFORMING THE MILITARY FOR THE 21ST CENTURY

The attacks of September 11, 2001, shattered many myths – among them, the illusion that the post-Cold War world would be one of extended peace that would allow America to stand down its forces and reduce defense spending.

The military President Bush inherited needed substantial investments in areas such as modernization and procurement – as well as training, health care, and quality of life for our troops and their families. When President Bush took office, 60 percent of all military housing was substandard. Many military facilities were dilapidated, and in urgent need of replacement or repair. Shipbuilding was far below levels needed to maintain the fleet. Many troops were not getting the training and flying time they needed to maintain readiness. The military did not have the capabilities needed for the 21st century.

During the 2000 campaign, George W. Bush promised the men and women of the Armed Forces: "help is on the way." Upon taking office, the Bush Administration began building a 21st century military that could protect America against the threats of a new era.

To win the war on terror, the Administration equipped our troops with real-time battlefield intelligence capabilities. The Defense Department expanded America's arsenal of unmanned aerial vehicles from fewer than 170 when the President took office to more than 6,000 today, including Air Force armed Predator drones.

The Administration expanded America's special operations forces so the military can respond more quickly to actionable intelligence on the terrorists who are in hiding. Over the past eight years, the Administration more than doubled funding for special operators, created the first-ever Marine special operations component within the U.S. Special Operations Command and gave Special Operations Command the lead role in the global war on terror.

The Administration placed a new focus on counterinsurgency. Under the direction of Generals Petraeus and Mattis, the Army and

Marine Corps published a new counterinsurgency manual. The central objectives of this counterinsurgency strategy are to secure the population, gain support of the people, and train local forces to take security responsibility on their own. The new strategy also stressed the importance of accompanying security gains with real benefits in people's daily lives. Today, every branch of the military receives the counterinsurgency training that was once reserved primarily for special operations forces.

In addition to making these changes to help our Armed Forces prevail in the war on terror, the Administration began transforming the military in early 2001 to confront other challenges that may emerge in the decades ahead. The Defense Department developed a new defense strategy that made preparing for surprise and uncertainty the centerpiece of U.S. defense planning.

The Defense Department moved funding from Cold War legacy programs – such as the Crusader artillery program and the Comanche helicopter program – to accelerate the development of transformational capabilities, including modern, networked, and expeditionary platforms. And the Administration invested $138 billion in transformational military capabilities, plus an additional half a trillion dollars in research and development so the Defense Department can build even more advanced capabilities in the decades ahead.

The Defense Department undertook the most sweeping transformation of America's global force posture since the end of the World War II. In 2004, the President announced that over the next decade, America would move its forces from Cold War garrisons in Europe and Asia, and reposition them so they can surge quickly to trouble spots anywhere in the world.

The President withdrew the United States from the ABM Treaty, and worked to develop the first system capable of protecting the homeland against the threat of ballistic missiles. In 2008, the United States signed agreements with Poland and the Czech Republic to establish missile defense sites on their territories, so we can protect America and our NATO allies from ballistic missile attacks emanating from the Middle East. The United States also began work with NATO on new capabilities to defend against short- and medium-range missile attacks from the Middle East.

The President also made historic nuclear reductions that were eventually codified in the Moscow Treaty, which commits the United States and Russia to reduce their operationally deployed strategic nuclear warheads to between 1,700 and 2,200 by 2012. Since the treaty took effect, the United States has reduced its operationally deployed strategic nuclear warheads from more than 6,000 when the President took office to fewer than 3,800 today. When the rest of the reductions are completed, the total U.S. nuclear stockpile will be one-quarter the size it was at the end of the Cold War, the lowest level since the Eisenhower Administration.

The President developed a new approach to strategic deterrence, through the Nuclear Posture Review, that reduces America's reliance on nuclear weapons without reducing America's deterrent. In place of the old Cold War "Triad" of sea, air, and land based nuclear weapons, the Nuclear Posture Review established a "New Triad" made up of reduced offensive nuclear forces, advanced conventional capabilities, and a range of new defenses (such as ballistic missile defense, cruise missile defense, space defense, and cyber defense) – all supported by a revitalized defense infrastructure. This New Triad is designed to better protect America and our allies from nuclear blackmail or attack.

The Administration also expanded, rebalanced, and transformed our military forces. Under the President's leadership, the size of America's Army and Marine Corps increased by 92,000 troops. In addition, the Defense Department took approximately 40,000 defense positions previously held by uniformed military personnel and put them in civilian hands – freeing up those troops for military tasks and assignments. The Administration launched a new Global Peacekeeping Operations Initiative – so we can better train foreign peacekeepers and relieve demand on American forces to perform these missions. These steps have made significantly more forces available for missions in the war on terror.

The President also launched the most significant reorganization of the Army in a generation – replacing the division-based structure with a 21st century structure built around "modular" brigade combat teams that are flexible and mobile. To help bring the Army into the 21st century, the Administration invested $18 billion to develop the Army's Future Combat System and invested $29 billion to equip and modernize the National Guard.

At the President's direction, the Navy established a new Fleet Response Plan that doubles the number of Carrier Strike Groups that can be deployed on short notice. The Administration initiated and completed the conversion of four Trident nuclear submarines into advanced conventional submarines that can silently carry special operations forces and cruise missiles within striking distance of our adversaries. The

Administration created new Expeditionary Air Wings that are more flexible and effective.

The President also helped lead a transformation of the NATO Alliance. Working with allies, he established a new "NATO Response Force" that allows the Alliance to deploy rapid reaction forces on short notice anywhere in the world, and transformed the NATO Command Structure, including the creation of a new NATO command to drive Alliance transformation. The President led the effort to bring seven new nations into the NATO Alliance, and rallied our allies to transform NATO from a defensive alliance focused on protecting Europe from Soviet tank invasion into a dynamic alliance that is now operating in Afghanistan, Baghdad, Kosovo, and Sudan. Because of the President's leadership, an Alliance some said had lost its purpose after the Cold War is now meeting the challenges of the 21st century.

Finally, the President invested in America's most important military asset – the men and women who wear our nation's uniform. Under the President's leadership, the Pentagon took steps to attract and retain talent in our Armed Forces, with targeted pay raises and quality of life improvements. The Administration spent $25 billion to improve military housing; funded the privatization of more than 193,000 family housing units; improved the way the military cares for the families of the fallen and implemented recommendations from the Dole-Shalala Commission; and issued new regulations that amended the Family Medical Leave Act to give military family members up to 26 weeks of protected leave – up from 12 weeks of normal family medical leave – to care for a service member injured in the line of duty. This protection was also extended to additional family members. Families of Guard and Reserve forces can now also take up to 12 weeks of protected leave to manage their affairs when a family member is called up for active duty.

In all, over the past eight years, the Bush Administration increased defense spending by $216 billion, a nearly 73 percent increase. Because of the President's actions, America is better prepared to fight today's war on terror – and we are better prepared for the new and still unknown challenges that almost certainly will emerge as the 21st century unfolds. President Bush will leave his successor with a stronger military. And the historic reforms he enacted will enhance the security of the American people for decades to come.

VETERANS

As the Administration transformed the Department of Defense, the President also provided historic support for our Nation's veterans. By the time he finished his eighth year in office, the President had increased funding for veterans' services by more than 98 percent.

The President increased the VA's medical care budget by 115 percent since 2001. Since 2001, the Administration helped more than 2 million more veterans take advantage of the VA health care system. Total outpatient visits increased from 44 million when the President took office to 70 million today, and the number of prescriptions filled grew from 98 million when the President took office to 130 million today. Between 2001 and 2006, the VA also reduced the backlog of disability claims pending more than 6 months at the end of each year by more than 50 percent. And the VA is currently processing veterans' disability claims on average approximately 50 days faster than they were in 2002.

The Administration focused these increased resources on veterans with service-related disabilities, low incomes, and special needs. The Administration spent more than $6 billion to modernize and expand VA medical facilities and build new facilities closer to our veterans' homes. Since 2001, the VA has opened 280 new community-based clinics. The Administration expanded grants to help homeless veterans, and as a result, the number of homeless veterans dropped nearly 40 percent between 2001 and 2007.

For more than a century, Federal law prohibited disabled veterans from receiving both their military retired pay and their VA disability compensation. The President believed that combat-injured and severely disabled veterans deserved better. So in 2003, he became the first President in more than 100 years to sign concurrent receipt legislation.

In February 2007, news broke about the deplorable living conditions some of our Nation's wounded warriors were experiencing at Walter Reed Army Medical Center. As soon as the conditions came to his attention, the President went to Walter Reed to visit our recovering troops. He said: "It is not right to have someone volunteer to wear our uniform and not get the best possible care. I apologize for what they went through, and we're going to fix the problem."

The Administration took immediate steps to follow through on the President's promise. The substandard building housing out-patients was shut down, and those living there were moved to quality housing. Those responsible for the failures at Walter Reed were held to account. And to ensure that wounded troops at Walter Reed and other facilities across America got the care they deserved, the President formed a bipartisan presidential commission, chaired by former Senator Bob Dole and former Secretary of Health and Human Services Donna Shalala. He asked this commission to review the care provided to service members from the time they leave the battlefield through their return to civilian life.

In July 2007, the Dole-Shalala Wounded Warriors Commission submitted specific recommendations for modernizing and improving our military and veteran systems of care. The Administration implemented all the commission's recommendations it could administratively. In October 2007, the President sent Congress legislation to implement those recommendations that required legislation. Many of these reforms were included in the 2008 National Defense Authorization Act.

In June 2008, the President signed legislation that included a significant expansion of the GI bill, including measures to allow our troops to transfer their unused education benefits to spouses or children.

The Administration also established a new National Center of Excellence in November 2007 to help pioneer new treatments and improve the diagnosis and care of traumatic brain injury and Post-Traumatic Stress Disorder.

In 2001, President Bush declared: "America's veterans honored their commitment to our country through their military service. I will honor our commitment to them." Over the past eight years, he worked to meet that pledge.

FOREIGN POLICY

Speaking at the Ronald Reagan Presidential Library in 1999, Governor Bush laid out the foreign policy vision that would guide his Administration. He said he would pursue a "distinctly American internationalism," promising to promote political liberty, free markets, and free trade, and to set clear priorities for America's engagement with the world.

Russia

When President Bush took office, he made clear his determination to transform the Russian-American relationship and put what he termed the "dead ideological rivalry" of the Cold War behind us. Some critics feared the President's agenda – his promise to withdraw from the ABM Treaty; his determination to build defenses to protect against ballistic missile attack; and his declared intention to strengthen and expand the NATO Alliance – meant that America and Russia were headed toward a new arms race. But when President Bush met President Putin for the first time in 2001 in Slovenia, the two presidents emerged from their discussions expressing confidence that the two countries could put past animosities behind them.

The two leaders held four meetings during President Bush's first year in office, culminating in a November 2001 summit where President Bush announced his intention to reduce the United States' operationally deployed strategic nuclear warheads by some two-thirds – to between 1,700 and 2,200 weapons. A few months later, President Putin made a similar commitment. The President later announced that America was withdrawing from the ABM Treaty, and President Putin declared that the decision "presents no threat to the security of the Russian Federation." Instead of the arms race critics had feared, the United States and Russia had both codified historic reductions in their deployed offensive nuclear arsenals in the Moscow Treaty five months later.

As President Bush helped end the era of adversarial arms control negotiations, the Administration worked to help integrate Russia into the diplomatic, political, economic, and security structures of the

West. Under the President's leadership, the NATO-Russia Council was established in May 2002. The Administration also worked to expand America's bilateral cooperation with Russia – including steps to prevent the spread of weapons of mass destruction; combat global terrorism; and advance economic and civil nuclear cooperation.

At the same time, the President made clear that the era of dividing lines and spheres of influence in Europe was over, and that the United States would work to remove the false boundaries that had divided the continent for too long. In a speech at Warsaw University in 2001, the President declared: "We will not trade away the fate of free European peoples: No more Munichs. No more Yaltas." Under the President's leadership, the NATO Alliance conducted two more rounds of expansion. And during the 2008 NATO Summit in Bucharest, he secured a commitment from NATO allies that in the future Georgia and Ukraine would be admitted into the Alliance. The Administration forged strategic relationships with newly independent nations in Central Asia and the Caucasus. The President increased energy cooperation with Turkey, Georgia, Azerbaijan, and the Caspian countries. And he built strategic relationships with nations like India, whose relationship with America had been strained for decades by Cold War tensions.

While the United States cast off Cold War thinking, leaders in Moscow had a harder time doing so. Despite the growing cooperation with the United States in many areas, Russian leaders continued to view the growing American relationships in Central Europe, Central Asia, and the Caucasus as threatening. Russia worked to block or delay the further expansion of NATO and threatened to target Poland and the Czech Republic with nuclear weapons because of their intention to host U.S. missile defense sites. Over time, Russia became increasingly authoritarian at home and aggressive abroad. In August 2008, Russia invaded Georgia, sending its forces across an internationally-recognized border. The Administration responded forcefully in support of Georgia's sovereignty, independence, and territorial integrity, and made clear that the United States and its allies would continue to resist any Russian attempt to consign free peoples to archaic "spheres of influence."

Over the past eight years, the Bush Administration sought to encourage the emergence of a strong, prosperous, and responsible Russia. Much good came from those efforts – including historic nuclear reductions, a seamless withdrawal from the ABM Treaty, and increasing Russian-American cooperation in the fight against terror and against the spread of weapons of mass destruction. Although there were important areas of cooperation, Russian leaders also made some poor choices that missed opportunities and eroded Russia's democratic progress.

India

During the Cold War, India's close economic and defense ties with the Soviet Union resulted in a strained relationship with the United States. While some progress in mending ties took place following the collapse of the USSR, relations were set back after India's 1998 nuclear tests resulted in the imposition of U.S. sanctions.

The President was determined to end the history of mistrust, and transform America's relationship with India into a strong strategic partnership. In September 2001, the President waived the sanctions imposed after India's 1998 nuclear test. And just weeks after the 9/11 terrorist attacks, he welcomed then-Indian Prime Minister Vajpayee to the White House, where the two leaders pledged cooperation in the fight against terror and agreed to work together to transform the relationship between their countries. During the next four years, the American and Indian governments worked to improve ties in education, agriculture, trade, high-technology, clean energy, civil space, and military-to-military relations.

On July 18, 2005, President Bush welcomed India's new Prime Minister, Manmohan Singh, to the White House. Both leaders declared their intention to forge a new era in relations and "establish a global partnership" between their two countries. Since that time, the United States and India have established a bilateral relationship that is closer than ever before.

During the Prime Minister's visit to Washington, the two leaders announced the creation of several high level initiatives to further the economic relationship. Partly as a result, U.S.-India trade increased by more than 300 percent between 2000 and 2007. And Indian foreign direct investment in the United States and U.S. investment in India have both reached all time highs.

Finally, the two countries signed an historic civil nuclear cooperation agreement, designed to end India's three decades of nuclear isolation following its first detonation of a nuclear device in 1974. Under the accord, India agreed to separate its civilian and military nuclear programs, and operate its entire civil nuclear energy program under the safeguards of the International Atomic Energy Agency and other international guidelines. The United States, in turn, agreed to work with its international partners to lift the three-decade moratorium on nuclear trade with India, and provide assistance to strengthen India's civil nuclear energy efforts. The two nations also agreed to strengthen non-proliferation cooperation to keep the world's most dangerous weapons out of the hands of terrorists.

In 2008, Congress passed, and the President signed, the United States-India Nuclear Cooperation Approval and Nonproliferation Enhancement Act. This agreement put the relationship between the United States and India on a new footing, and established a level of cooperation between the world's two largest democracies that would have been hard to imagine in prior decades. The President achieved all this, while at the same time forging an unprecedented level of coopera-tion with Pakistan.

On his final visit to see President Bush at the White House in Sep-tember 2008, Prime Minister Singh declared, "there has been a massive transformation of India-United States relations.... And when history is written, I think it will be recorded that President George W. Bush made an historic goal in bringing our two democracies closer to each other."

China

Before President Bush took office, America's policy in Asia had become too focused on China, to the detriment of America's alliances with partners such as Japan, South Korea, Thailand, the Philippines, and Australia.

During his 2000 campaign, the President described the approach his Administration would take toward China, declaring: "China is a competitor, not a strategic partner. We must deal with China without ill-will, but without illusions." He pledged to cooperate with China in areas such as expanding trade, preventing the spread of weapons of mass destruction, and attaining peace on the Korean peninsula. But he made clear that, as President, he would speak out for human rights and that he would "show American power and purpose in strong support for our Asian friends and allies – for democratic South Korea across the Yellow Sea; for democratic Japan and the Philippines across the China seas; for democratic Australia and Thailand." He continued: "[T]his [also] means honoring our promise to the people of Taiwan. We do not deny there is one China. But we deny the right of Beijing to impose their rule on a free people. As I've said before, we will help Taiwan to defend itself."

Months into his presidency, an unarmed U.S. Navy EP-3 aircraft was intercepted by a Chinese jet fighter in international airspace, had its nose cone sheared off and a propeller clipped by the Chinese aircraft, and was forced to make an emergency landing on the Chinese island of Hainan. The American crew was detained by Chinese authorities for 11 days before the new Administration secured their release and the eventual return of the American plane. The President's handling of the EP-3 crisis showed the Chinese leadership that the new Administration would be tough in defending America's national interests, but that it was also willing to negotiate to defuse disagreements.

With the crisis behind them, President Bush began working to build a constructive, cooperative, consistent, and candid relationship with Chinese leaders. He chose to attend the APEC leaders meeting in Shanghai just days after the 9/11 terrorist attacks. The Chinese leadership responded by offering cooperation in the war on terror. The President used this opportunity to build good relations with China's leaders and to encourage China to play a constructive and peaceful role in the world.

In 2005, he established a new Senior Dialogue – a regular high-level exchange on global areas of mutual concern, including North Korea, the Middle East, Africa, and Latin America. In 2006, he established a new Strategic Economic Dialogue with China, where economic leaders from both nations meet to discuss ways to ensure long-term growth and widely-shared prosperity in both economies – as well as address issues like exchange rates, environmental protection, and intellectual property rights. As he increased America's engagement with Beijing, the President also worked to transform America's military capabilities and to strengthen military cooperation with America's friends in the Asia-Pacific.

This approach produced results in a number of areas. On Taiwan, the President's leadership helped place the cross-Strait relationship on a more stable and positive course. In 2001, the Administration announced a robust arms sales package to Taiwan, and the President publicly stated his willingness to defend Taiwan if it were attacked. He also reaffirmed America's commitment to the one China policy, and publicly declared that the United States does not support Taiwan independence and opposes any "unilateral changes in the status quo . . . by either side."

This helped to ease China's concerns that the United States was secretly supporting Taiwan's independence and gave China the confidence to subtly adjust its Taiwan policies. President Hu Jintao altered China's policy from an emphasis on early reunification to a policy of long-term patience. In March 2008, the election of President Ma in Taiwan gave the two sides a chance to ease tensions. After a nine-year hiatus, leaders from both sides met and concluded agreements to allow direct trade, air travel, shipping, and mail service between the mainland and Taiwan, and to allow mainland tourists to visit Taiwan. Because of the President's engagement of Beijing and his strong support for the people of Taiwan, cross-Strait tensions have diminished significantly during his time in office.

On North Korea, President Bush persuaded China to play a leadership role in the effort to achieve a Korean peninsula free of nuclear weapons. Early in his Administration, the President made clear that North Korea was not solely an American problem, but rather a Northeast Asian problem that America was willing to help solve through multilateral diplomacy. China responded positively to this change in strategy. In October 2002, Chinese President Jiang Zemin visited the President's ranch in Crawford, where he stated for the first time that China unequivocally agreed that the Korean peninsula must be denuclearized. In August 2003, Beijing hosted the first round of the Six-Party Talks – which eventually produced an agreement by North Korea to abandon its nuclear weapons and nuclear program.

When, in October 2006, North Korea broke its agreement and conducted a nuclear test, China stood with the United States and supported the passage of a Chapter VII resolution in the UN Security Council. The United States convinced China to place economic pressure on North Korea, which helped bring the North Koreans back to the negotiating table in December 2006. In February 2007, North Korea agreed to halt plutonium production at its Yongbyon nuclear facility. And later that year, North Korea began disabling its main plutonium production and reprocessing facilities. In June 2008, North Korea submitted a nuclear declaration to China and blew up the cooling tower of its nuclear reactor at Yongbyon. Much work remains, but an important change has taken place over the past eight years. When President Bush took office, denuclearization was viewed as an issue between the United States and North Korea. Today, it is seen as a challenge for which the United States, China, and the other nations in the region all share responsibility.

The President's decision to attend the Beijing Olympics in his final year in office made a strong impression on Chinese leaders. Yet ten months before the Olympics, President Bush also became the first American president to meet publicly with His Holiness the Dalai Lama. Before leaving for Beijing, the President hosted a meeting at the White House with Chinese dissidents and democracy activists. And while in Beijing, the President visited a Protestant church to underscore his support for religious freedom.

The President leaves office with the American relationship with China on a strong and stable footing. Tensions between Washington and Beijing have dissipated, cross-Strait tensions have also eased, and China is playing a more constructive role on the international stage. And all this has been achieved while the President simultaneously stood with the people of Taiwan, spoke out forcefully for human rights, democracy, and religious liberty in China, and strengthened America's ties with our allies in the Asia Pacific.

Asia-Pacific Cooperation

America has five treaty alliances in the Asia Pacific – and during his eight years in office, President Bush bolstered each one.

When the President took office, America's relations with Japan were frayed by trade disputes, differences over North Korea, and tensions over U.S. bases and troops in Okinawa. The President began working immediately to strengthen this vital alliance. As part of his global force posture review, the President began a relocation of U.S. forces in Japan – moving U.S airbases from urban to rural areas, and beginning the transition of more than 8,000 Marines from Okinawa to Guam. The Pentagon significantly expanded U.S. military cooperation with Japan – working with Japan to jointly develop ballistic missile defenses and reaching an agreement to home-base a nuclear-powered aircraft carrier in Japan for the first time starting in 2008. After the 9/11 attacks, Prime Minister Koizumi deployed Japanese Self Defense Forces in both Afghanistan and Iraq. Today, the U.S.-Japan relationship is stronger than it has been at any time since the end of World War II.

In South Korea, when the President took office, there was growing public opposition to the presence of American troops on the Korean peninsula. So as part of the global force posture review, the President set in motion a plan to move American troops out of cities and towns and into more strategically effective positions – consolidating our military presence into two hubs south of the Han River, and preparing to transfer war fighting operational control to the Republic of Korea in 2012. In 2007, the Administration signed a free trade agreement with South Korea that is projected to add more than $10 billion annually to our economy if approved by Congress. And the Administration finalized South Korea's entry into the Visa Waiver Program – expanding opportunities for travel and trade between the two nations.

When the President took office, relations with Australia had been damaged by the imposition of a tariff rate quota on certain agricultural products in 1999. Upon taking office in 2001, the President moved quickly to lift this tariff-rate quota. After the 9/11 attacks, Australia invoked the ANZUS treaty, which commits the countries to each others' defense, for the first time. Australian forces joined American forces from the very first moments of combat in both Afghanistan and Iraq, and have fought side-by-side with American troops throughout the war on terror. In 2004, the Administration signed a free trade agreement with Australia which went into effect in January 2005. And in September 2007, the President traveled to Sydney for the APEC summit, where he signed a landmark Defense Trade Treaty with Australia that will enhance defense and security cooperation between the two nations.

In 2003, the President declared Thailand a "Major Non-NATO Ally" of the United States – one of only 14 countries in the world so designated – putting them on par with other U.S. alliances in the region. Thailand has sent troops to both Afghanistan and Iraq, and opened its air bases to help coordinate the humanitarian response to the 2004 tsunami and the 2008 cyclone that devastated Burma. The Administration also provided $36 million to Thailand under the President's Emergency Plan for AIDS Relief. When the elected government in Thailand was overthrown in a 2006 military coup, the Administration made clear that Thailand's relationship with the United States could only be normalized with the restoration of democracy. Thailand's democratic elections in 2007 made that possible.

In the Philippines, when the President took office, a violent Islamic extremist terrorist group called Abu Sayyaf was highly active. The President worked to help the Philippines strengthen its armed forces for the fight against these terrorists. In 2003, he welcomed President Arroyo to the White House and announced that the United States had designated the Philippines a Major Non-NATO Ally. Later that year, he traveled to Manila where he became the first President since Eisenhower to address the Philippine Congress, announcing a new Defense Reform Program to help the Philippines upgrade its military capabilities. With American assistance, Filipino forces launched a campaign to combat terrorism. The United States also helped the Filipino government deliver aid to Muslim communities in the Southern Philippines that the terrorists had exploited – building roads, bridges, schools, and health clinics, and providing micro-credit to help local entrepreneurs.

As the President revitalized our major treaty alliances and created new ones, he also forged deeper ties with other free nations in Asia.

In Indonesia, the President advanced America's relationship with a nation that is home to more Muslims than any other. The President helped Indonesia's elected government develop the institutions of a vibrant democracy after decades under military rule. The United States launched a $157 million initiative to improve basic education in primary and junior secondary schools. When a tsunami hit the region in 2004, the United States rallied nations to provide relief to devastated communities in Indonesia. The United States and Indonesia also forged close cooperation in the war on terror, which helped foil a plot by the Southeast Asia terrorist network Jemaah Islamiyah and al Qaeda operatives to hijack an airplane and fly it into the Library Tower in Los Angeles. Today, the Jemaah Islamiyah network has been severely weakened. As a result of all these steps, America's relationship with Indonesia is stronger than it has been in decades – and the American people are safer as a result.

The Bush Administration also strengthened America's relations with Singapore, signing a free trade agreement that went into effect in January 2004. In 2005, President Bush signed a landmark Strategic Framework Agreement between the two nations – the most extensive security cooperation agreement ever signed with the Singapore government – giving the U.S. military a secure, reliable transit and logistics capacity at the heart of one of the most active strategic shipping lanes in the world.

The President also strengthened America's relations with Vietnam. He supported Vietnam's successful bid to join the World Trade Organization, and expanded trade between the two nations, which now tops $12 billion annually. He also provided over $230 million to Vietnam under the Emergency Plan for AIDS Relief. At the same time, he spoke out forcefully for the human rights and religious freedom of the Vietnamese people.

Speaking in Bangkok in August 2008, the President said: "When I became President, I brought a conviction that America is a Pacific nation – and that our interests and ideals require stronger engagement in Asia than ever before." During his eight years in office, the President achieved something many experts thought impossible: improving America's relationships with all of Asia's major powers simultaneously.

Western Hemisphere

When the President took office, democracy in Latin America was showing considerable signs of strain. Following the end of the Cold War, the region had seen a dramatic expansion of freedom as communist dictatorships and military regimes alike gave way to the advance of liberty. Yet despite these advances, millions in the hemisphere were shut off from the promise of this new century. Young democracies struggled to combat poverty, crime, and hopelessness – and this undermined the faith of many in the ability of democracy to improve their lives.

Populist demagogues in the region took advantage of this situation to advance increasingly authoritarian rule. They blamed poverty on free market economic reforms and American influence in the region – and promised to usher in a new era of socialism and a more equitable redistribution of wealth.

The President worked to help strengthen young democracies in the region against this new brand of populism, and to build government institutions that were fair, effective, and free of corruption. Since 2001, the Administration signed Millennium Challenge Compacts with Honduras, Nicaragua, and El Salvador, and Threshold Agreements with Guyana, Paraguay, and Peru, and determined Colombia to be eligible for a Compact. These agreements have committed nearly $930 million in new aid to support democracy, good governance, and development.

This new aid comes on top of the standard bilateral assistance that the United States provided. When the President came into office, the United States was sending approximately $860 million a year in foreign aid to Latin America and the Caribbean. By 2007, the Administration had increased this assistance to $1.6 billion. Altogether, the President sent a total of $8.5 billion to the region during his Administration – with a special focus on programs that help the poor.

The focus of this effort was to help young democracies in the region to advance social justice by improving conditions for their people. Since 2004, the United States has provided more than $300 million for education programs throughout the region. The President also deployed the USNS Comfort and humanitarian missions to Latin America, providing medical treatment to more than 100,000 people. The Administration worked to improve housing, providing more than $1 billion through the Overseas Private Investment Corporation to help expand the availability of affordable housing for working families in Latin America. The Administration worked with its G-8 partners to reduce the debt of Latin American and Caribbean nations by $4.8 billion and worked with the Inter-American Development Bank to cancel an additional $3.4 billion owed by some of the poorest countries in our hemisphere. Since 2002, the Administration has devoted more than $250 million to help the region's entrepreneurs with micro-credit loans and other assistance for people starting up small businesses, and worked to open new opportunities for the region's entrepreneurs through trade and investment. The President secured Congressional approval of new free trade agreements with Chile, five Central American nations and the Dominican Republic, and Peru. The Administration also signed free trade agreements with Colombia and Panama, both of which have not yet been approved by Congress.

The Bush Administration partnered with young democracies in the region to fight the scourge of drugs, by working to reduce the U.S. demand for drugs, working to intercept illegal drugs before they reach this country, and working with America's friends in the region to take on the drug trade. In 2007, the President committed the United States to the Merida Initiative – a partnership with Mexico and Central America to help keep narcotics off the streets and help those nations break the power and impunity of drug trafficking organizations.

Authoritarian populists did make some gains, with the elections of Evo Morales in Bolivia and Daniel Ortega in Nicaragua. Like Hugo Chavez in Venezuela, these leaders are working to disband institutions that limit their authority and replace them with new constitutions or laws that limit or silence their political opponents. But the forces of authoritarian populism saw setbacks as well. Alan Garcia defeated a Chavez ally in Peru's presidential election, and voters rejected Hugo Chavez's efforts to rewrite Venezuela's constitution – a setback to his efforts to consolidate control over Venezuela's political life.

The Bush Administration also built strong partnerships with democratic leaders across the region, including President Luis Ignacio Lula da Silva of Brazil; President Tabare Vazquez of Uruguay; President Michelle

Bachelet of Chile; President Antonio Saca of El Salvador; President Martin Torrijos of Panama; President Alvaro Colom of Guatemala; and President Fernando Lugo of Paraguay. Through the Security and Prosperity Partnership and the North American Leaders' Summit process, the President worked to increase cooperation with Canada and Mexico. In most countries in the hemisphere, democratic government was strengthened and institutionalized over the past eight years – and the popular consensus in favor of moderate, responsible political and economic policies has held. By his efforts to strengthen young democracies and help them deliver a better life for their people, President Bush helped lay the foundations for a strong democratic future in the Americas – and gave responsible leaders the tools they need to defend freedom and combat authoritarian populism.

Colombia

One of the major success stories in the Western Hemisphere is Colombia. In the 1990s, Colombia was on the verge of becoming a failed state, and possibly a narco-state. Some progress had been made under Plan Colombia – a 1999 agreement to expand counter-drug activities, modernize the military, strengthen the economy, and reform Colombia's political and judicial systems. To build on this progress, the Bush Administration expanded U.S. assistance to Colombia. The Administration re-designated the Marxist Revolutionary Armed Forces of Colombia (FARC) and the National Liberation Army as foreign terrorist organizations, and did the same for the right-wing paramilitary alliance, the United Self Defense Forces of Colombia. In 2002, Congress approved the use of American funds to support Colombian efforts against these groups.

The 2002 election of President Alvaro Uribe transformed the struggle for Colombia's future. President Uribe took bold stands to defend our shared democratic values and fight the scourges of drugs, crime, terror, and human rights abuses. To support his efforts, the Administration has provided more than $5 billion in assistance to Colombia. President Uribe's determined leadership has turned Colombia around. Since he took office, the Colombian Government reports that homicides have dropped by 40 percent, kidnappings by more than 80 percent, and terrorist attacks by more than 70 percent. Tens of thousands of paramilitary members have been demobilized. More than 10,000 members of the FARC have deserted. Colombia's economy recovered and grew by

7.5 percent in 2007. In July 2008, members of the Colombian military infiltrated the FARC and rescued 15 hostages, including three Americans who had been held captive for more than five years. The government has established its presence for the first time in all municipalities and is delivering services to better the lives of the Colombian people.

To support President Uribe and expand markets for American goods and services, in November 2006 the United States signed a free trade agreement with Colombia. Unfortunately, Congress did not vote on the agreement. But the transformation that has taken place in Colombia is remarkable. President Uribe and his fellow citizens have built Colombia into a strong democracy, a determined partner in the fight against drugs and terror, and one of America's strongest allies in the Western Hemisphere.

Cuba

The President's policy towards Cuba sought to help the Cuban people hasten an end to the Castro dictatorship and assist in that country's transition to a democratic society, governed by leaders freely chosen by the people in fair elections. In challenging the regime, the Administration expanded initiatives to empower the Cuban people, strengthen the democratic opposition, break the Castro regime's information blockade, and deny revenues to the dictatorship. In 2002, the President proposed his Initiative for a New Cuba, which offered to liberalize U.S. restrictions on travel and trade in response to political and economic reforms, including free elections for already-scheduled Cuban National Assembly elections. The Cuban regime rejected these offers to change the U.S.-Cuba relationship.

From 2001 to 2008, the Administration provided more than $300 million in assistance to promote democracy in Cuba. Of this amount, more than $125 million was for activities to directly support emerging civil society movements in Cuba. The President also directed a substantial increase in U.S. efforts to get uncensored information to the Cuban people, primarily through Radio and TV Marti, which are now broadcast from aircraft and via satellite television as well as on a variety of AM and shortwave frequencies.

To show his support for Cuban democracy, the President had numerous meetings with Cuban dissidents – including those on the island through video teleconferences. And in 2007, the President bestowed the Presidential Medal of Freedom on Dr. Oscar Elias Biscet, a political prisoner, in recognition of Dr. Biscet's advocacy of non-violent democratic change in Cuba and to honor all courageous Cubans who have attempted to exercise their fundamental human rights.

Ending Conflicts in Africa

When President Bush took office, several wars were raging in Africa. The President worked with regional leaders and international organizations to end these wars and bring peace and new hope to war-ravaged lands. In Liberia, the Administration worked with the international community to remove Charles Taylor from power, paving the way for free elections in which Ellen Johnson Sirleaf became the first woman elected President on the continent of Africa. The United States also worked closely with South Africa to end a destructive civil war in the Democratic Republic of the Congo, and to support the Congo's first free and fair elections in more than 40 years.

In Sudan, the Administration helped broker a peace agreement between the government and the Sudan People's Liberation Movement (SPLM). The United States supported the deployment of a robust UN peacekeeping force in southern Sudan to help implement the agreement, and has provided more than $2 billion in humanitarian, development, and security sector reform assistance.

Just as peace was coming to southern Sudan, another conflict broke out in the west, where rebel groups in Darfur attacked government outposts. The government in Khartoum unleashed a horse-mounted militia called the Janjaweed, which carried out systematic assaults against innocent civilians. The human toll was staggering – more than 200,000 people died from the conflict or from malnutrition and disease that spread in its wake. And more than two million people were forced from their homes and villages into camps both inside and outside their country.

The President called the events in Darfur what they were: genocide. To relieve suffering in Darfur, the Administration has devoted more than $2 billion in humanitarian relief and development assistance since the conflict began – making the United States the world's largest donor to the people of Darfur. The Administration also worked to reach a peace agreement to end the conflict in Darfur, so the families of this troubled region could return safely to their homes and rebuild their lives in peace. In May 2006, an agreement was reached. Unfortunately, the Sudanese government of President Bashir refused to end its support of the Janjaweed, or allow the deployment of the UN-African

Union peacekeeping force called for in the agreement. So in May 2007, President Bush announced that the United States was moving ahead with extensive sanctions. Khartoum relented and agreed to the deployment of peacekeepers in Darfur. In July 2007, the UN Security Council voted unanimously to authorize the creation of the first hybrid UN-AU peacekeeping mission. So far, 10,000 of the 26,000-person force have been deployed. When fully mobilized, the UN-AU Mission in Darfur (UNAMID) will be the largest peacekeeping force in the world – and it represents the best chance for peace and security in Darfur.

Middle East Peace

When President Bush took office, the Israeli-Palestinian conflict was descending rapidly into a second intifada. Camp David II and subsequent negotiations had collapsed. The Palestinian leadership remained compromised by terror and corruption. The populations in Israel and the Palestinian Territories were not prepared for compromise. There was no consensus in Israel on the need to withdraw from the West Bank and Gaza. And large portions of the Palestinian population refused to accept the existence of Israel.

President Bush made two vital changes to U.S. policy. First, he became the first American president to call for a Palestinian state as a matter of policy. Second, while previous administrations had focused their attention on the contours of a future Palestinian state, the President shifted the focus to the character of a future Palestinian state. He refused to deal with the Palestinian leadership under Yasser Arafat and called for new leaders uncompromised by terror. And he committed to help the Palestinians build the political, economic, and security institutions of a democratic Palestinian state even before its borders had been defined.

Speaking in the Rose Garden on June 24, 2002, the President declared: "My vision is two states, living side by side in peace and security. There is simply no way to achieve that peace until all parties fight terror.... Peace requires a new and different Palestinian leadership, so that a Palestinian state can be born." He cautioned that "[a]ll who are familiar with the history of the Middle East realize that there may be setbacks in this process. Trained and determined killers, as we have seen, want to stop it." But, the President said, "If liberty can blossom in the rocky soil of the West Bank and Gaza, it will inspire millions of men and women around the globe who are equally weary of poverty and oppression, equally entitled to the benefits of democratic government.... This moment is both an opportunity and a test for all parties in the Middle East: an opportunity to lay the foundations for future peace; a test to show who is serious about peace and who is not."

With these changes in policy, the President identified terrorism as the primary obstacle to peace in the Middle East and the achievement of a Palestinian state. He sought to discredit and delegitimize terror, and make clear that a Palestinian state would never be born of it. And he supported the Israeli government's right to defend its people from attack, which gave Israelis confidence that they could not be forced into negotiations by terrorist tactics.

The United States organized the Red Sea Summit, held in June 2003. First, the President met in Sharm el-Sheikh, Egypt, with the leaders of Jordan, Saudi Arabia, Egypt, Bahrain, and the Palestinian Territories, who gathered to express their support for a performance-based, step-by-step plan for peace called "The Roadmap." Then, the President brought together Israeli and Palestinian leaders in Aqaba, on the Jordanian coast, where he launched direct discussions on implementing the Roadmap. At Aqaba, Prime Minister Sharon pledged to work toward an end to Israeli rule over Palestinians and toward the establishment of a Palestinian state. Palestinian Prime Minister Mahmoud Abbas pledged "a complete end to violence and terrorism." And both leaders formally accepted the benchmarks laid out in the Roadmap.

In the spring of 2004, Prime Minister Sharon made the decision to disengage from the West Bank and Gaza. The Israeli government also built a defensive barrier to protect Israeli citizens from terrorist attack, which produced in an immediate drop in terrorist incidents in Israel.

In November 2004, Arafat died. In January 2005, Prime Minister Abbas was elected as President of the Palestinian Authority. The end of the Arafat era and the election of a new Palestinian leader opposed to terror created new opportunities to help the Palestinian people develop their economy and build the institutions of a democratic state. The United States responded to this development by increasing assistance to the Palestinian Authority, and urging other governments to do the same.

By the fall of 2005, Israel had withdrawn all Israeli Defense Forces and nearly 8,000 settlers from Gaza, returning control of that territory to the Palestinian people. Israel also withdrew from parts of the northern West Bank. With the help of the United States, Israeli and Palestinian leaders reached an Agreement on Movement and Access so Palestinians could realize the benefits of that withdrawal.

In January 2006, Prime Minister Sharon suffered a massive stroke that incapacitated one of the key leaders driving the movement toward peace. He was succeeded by Deputy Prime Minister Ehud Olmert. That same month, the peace process suffered another setback when Hamas narrowly won Palestinian elections with slightly more than 44 percent of the vote. The vote was seen more as a rejection of the past than an endorsement of Hamas – but it put Hamas in control of the Palestinian Legislative Council and the Prime Minister's Office.

Some had counseled putting off the elections. The President disagreed. He explained his decision in a speech to the American Legion a month after the Palestinian vote: "It should come as no surprise that after 60 years of Western nations excusing and accommodating the lack of freedom in the Middle East, civil society in that region is not strong and those with the most extreme views are the most organized. It will take time for the people of this region to build political parties and movements that are moderate in their views and capable of competing in a free democratic system. Yet free elections cannot wait for perfect conditions. Free elections are instruments of change. By giving people an opportunity to organize, express their views, and change the existing order, elections strengthen the forces of freedom and encourage citizens to take control of their own destiny."

In June 2007, Hamas led a coup against President Abbas' government and seized control of the Gaza Strip. President Abbas expelled Hamas from the Palestinian government and declared a state of emergency. He named Salam Fayyad as the new Prime Minister. The new Palestinian leadership was quickly recognized by the United States, the European Union, and Israel. The Palestinian territories were now effectively divided, with Hamas in control of the Gaza Strip and the Palestinian Authority in control of the West Bank. But the Hamas leadership was now isolated by the international community, and the Palestinian government now had two leaders who opposed terror, and understood that violence is the enemy of the Palestinian people and their hopes for a Palestinian state.

On July 16, 2007, President Bush announced that the advent of new Palestinian leadership committed to fighting terror and to a peaceful resolution of the Israeli-Palestinian conflict created the conditions necessary to reinvigorate peace efforts. He said that the United States had lifted financial restrictions that had been placed on the Palestinian Authority after Hamas took power and announced new measures to support Palestinian businesses and help reform the Palestinian security services. And he called for a conference in the fall of 2007 that would include Israelis, Palestinians, and nations in the region that support the creation of a Palestinian state.

Through concerted diplomacy, Arab leaders were persuaded to be a part of the process at its inception. In November 2007, the Annapolis Conference was convened. This conference, and the Paris conference that followed a month later, launched a new peace effort, and secured international and regional support for bilateral negotiations, Palestinian institution-building, the fulfillment of Roadmap obligations, and greater Arab outreach to Israel.

Palestinian and Israeli negotiators met throughout 2008, including more than a dozen meetings between Prime Minister Olmert and President Abbas. At the same time, an American-led mission began to train and equip Palestinian security forces to make them more capable in the fight against violence and terror. The President traveled to the region in January 2008 and again in May, and Secretary Rice made several trips as well. Former British Prime Minister Tony Blair, who was serving as the envoy to the Middle East for the Quartet (the United States, Russia, the European Union, and the United Nations), worked with Israelis and Palestinians to promote economic growth in the West Bank and build the institutions of a future Palestinian state. Negotiations toward the creation of that state were slowed by a political crisis in Israel that eventually led to the resignation of Israeli Prime Minister Olmert.

As the President prepared to leave office, no peace agreement had been reached. However, President Bush leaves an improved situation, and one that represents an opportunity for the new Administration. Despite the control of Gaza by Hamas terrorists – and rocket and mortar attacks against Israel in December 2008 that forced Israel to launch retaliatory action against Hamas – the Israeli security situation has been improved over the past eight years. These security improvements have given Israelis the confidence they need to negotiate. The Palestinian people have new leaders in the Palestinian Authority who reject terror and seek peace with Israel. Palestinian leaders in the West Bank have made progress toward building the governing and security institutions of a future state. Israel has withdrawn all settlers from Gaza. Both Israeli and Palestinian leaders have accepted the principle of territorial compromise. Both sides have agreed to a Roadmap for the eventual creation of a Palestinian state. Arab leaders are actively supporting the peace process. And the United States, Israel, and the Palestinians have all agreed on a common goal: an independent, democratic, viable Palestinian state that lives side-by-side with Israel in security and peace.

The Broader Freedom Agenda

The advance of liberty is an essential part of the President's strategy to protect America in the war on terror – yet the freedom agenda is much more than that. The President believes that standing with those struggling for freedom, and helping those suffering from conditions of hopelessness, is something ingrained in the character of our Nation. And even if the 9/11 attacks had never happened, President Bush would have been a steadfast champion of freedom's cause across the globe.

Indeed, the President's first speech on the freedom agenda came nearly three months before 9/11. In June 2001, he traveled to Europe and spoke to the students and faculty at Warsaw University. He stated that tyrants, however brutal, are "ultimately defenseless against determined men and women armed only with their conscience and their faith." He promised to stand with "[e]very European nation that struggles toward democracy and free markets" and ensure these nations have the opportunity to join the institutions of Europe. He pledged to support the advance of democracy in the Balkans and set the goal of a Europe "without Brezhnev, and Honecker, and Ceausescu and, yes, without Milosevic." He promised to support Ukraine's democracy, and to work for the day when Russia's "greatness [is] measured by the strength of its democracy." And he called on Europe's new democracies to aid the cause of liberty and prosperity in Africa and other struggling corners of the world, declaring: "Those who have benefited and prospered most from the commitment to freedom and openness have an obligation to help others that are seeking their way along that path."

The events of 9/11 only confirmed the President's belief that the expansion of liberty is essential to peace. As he put it in his address to Congress immediately after the 9/11 attacks: "Freedom and fear are at war. The advance of human freedom – the great achievement of our time, and the great hope of every time – now depends on us." For the President, the 9/11 attacks resolved the long-standing debate between "realist" and "idealist" schools of American foreign policy, as it became clear that supporting the expansion of freedom and democracy in the

Middle East was the only realistic way to ensure the long-term security of the country.

In a November 2003 speech on the 20th anniversary of the National Endowment for Democracy, President Bush pledged to work for freedom in "outposts of oppression" such as such as Belarus, Burma, Cuba, Iran, North Korea, Syria, and Zimbabwe. He promised to speak out for freedom in China and to show to China's leaders that, ultimately, "freedom is indivisible – that social and religious freedom is also essential to national greatness and national dignity." He said that the "focus of American policy for decades to come" must be the advance of liberty in the Middle East and declared: "60 years of excusing and accommodating the lack of freedom in the Middle East did nothing to make us safe." He concluded: "The advance of freedom is the calling of our time, and the calling of our country."

During his eight years in office, the President backed these words with concrete actions. He expanded Federal support for democrats and reformers across the world. When the President took office, the Federal Government devoted approximately $700 million to democracy, governance, and human rights programs. Working with Congress, the President increased that funding during his presidency to $1.1 billion in 2008. The budget for the National Endowment for Democracy more than tripled during his Presidency. And he transformed the way we deliver development aid by creating the Millennium Challenge Account to support developing nations that govern justly, invest in their people, open up their economies, and make democratic reforms.

The President enshrined the freedom agenda in the national security policy of the United States. His 2002 National Security Strategy declared that the "values of freedom are right and true for every person, in every society – and .... [t]he United States will use this moment of opportunity to extend the benefits of freedom across the globe." His 2006 National Security Strategy declared: "It is the policy of the United States to seek and support democratic movements and institutions in every nation and culture, with the ultimate goal of ending tyranny in our world.... Championing freedom advances our interests because the survival of liberty at home increasingly depends on the success of liberty abroad.... The advance of freedom and human dignity through democracy is the long-term solution to the transnational terrorism of today."

As he took these steps, the President reached out directly to those struggling against tyranny and oppression, meeting personally with more than 180 dissidents and democratic activists from more than 35 countries. He became the first President to meet in the White House with democracy activists from China, and the first President to meet publicly with the Dalai Lama. In 2007, the President traveled to Prague to attend an international conference of dissidents and democracy activists. And to show America's support for these brave reformers, the President announced in Prague that his Administration was directing every U.S. ambassador in an un-free nation to seek out and meet with activists for democracy and human rights.

The President rallied the world's free nations to support democratic change. In 2005, the United States and India worked together to create a new United Nations Democracy Fund – which for the first time explicitly committed the United Nations to promoting democratic governance. At the 2007 APEC Summit in Sydney, the President joined with Australia, Japan, South Korea, Indonesia, the Philippines, and Canada to launch the new Asia-Pacific Democracy Partnership – the first organization in the region dedicated to promoting and strengthening democracy. In Iraq, the President assembled a coalition to help that young democracy defend itself against terrorists and extremists. And in Afghanistan, the President worked with other leaders to secure a commitment from the NATO Alliance to take over the International Security Assistance Force – and today personnel from all 26 NATO allies and 17 partner nations are on the ground, helping the Afghan people secure their democracy and rebuild their country.

The President stood with those who demanded democratic change in the Orange Revolution in Ukraine; the Rose Revolution in Georgia; the Tulip Revolution in Kyrgyzstan; and the Cedar Revolution in Lebanon. The President urged Pakistani President Musharraf to allow free elections and used America's influence to support the peaceful transition of power and the expansion of democracy in one of our country's most important allies in the war on terror. The President supported Kosovo as it established itself as an independent nation and Europe's newest democracy. The President helped broker an end to conflicts in Africa, and with his support the Democratic Republic of the Congo held the first multiparty elections in four decades; Sierra Leone held free elections and saw its first peaceful transfer of power to the democratic opposition; and Liberia held free elections after decades of civil strife.

The President also supported and encouraged America's friends and allies in the Middle East as they began to respond to the desires of their people for greater liberty and self-government. During his time in office, the United Arab Emirates held elections for its Federal National Council. Algeria held its first competitive Presidential elections. Kuwait held elections in which women were allowed to vote and hold office for the first time. Citizens voted in municipal elections in Saudi Arabia, in competitive parliamentary elections in Jordan, Morocco, and Bahrain, and in a multiparty Presidential election in Yemen.

Amid this progress, there were also setbacks for democracy during the President's time in office. Egypt held a contested presidential election – but then jailed the opposition party candidate. After the Cedar Revolution, Syria sowed political instability in Lebanon, and Hezbollah turned its weapons on Lebanese citizens. Russia grew increasingly authoritarian, and launched an invasion of Georgia. In 2007, Mauritania elected its first democratic government in free and fair elections since 1960, but a year later that government was overthrown in a coup. And there has been democratic backsliding in Venezuela, Bolivia, Ecuador, and Nicaragua.

Despite these setbacks, the cause of liberty made enormous progress during President Bush's time in office. In the past eight years, tens of millions of human beings have joined the ranks of the free.

Transformational Diplomacy

To advance the cause of freedom, the President transformed the tools of American diplomacy for the challenges of a new century. The Administration revolutionized the civilian role in counterinsurgency with the creation of Provincial Reconstruction Teams, or PRTs, in Afghanistan and Iraq. PRTs bring together civilian, diplomatic, and military personnel, and move into communities that the military has cleared of terrorists to consolidate the peace. In Afghanistan, for example, PRTs have built roads and bridges, rehabilitated schools, and raised literacy rates. In Iraq, PRTs have mentored District Councils in Baghdad; brokered a settlement that brought Sunnis back into the Kirkuk Provincial Council after a year-long boycott; and helped establish a Major Crimes Court in Ninewa province.

The President also recognized that, in the years ahead, civilian expertise will be needed in other countries where we do not have ongoing military operations. So in 2004, the Bush Administration created a new Office of Reconstruction and Stabilization in the State Department. This new office is charged with coordinating the Federal Government's civilian efforts to respond to crises in failed and post-conflict states, and to help build the political, economic, and administrative institutions that can be the basis of a durable peace.

One of the lessons learned from the experience in Iraq was that while military personnel can be rapidly deployed anywhere in the world, the same is not true of U.S. Government civilians. So the Office of Reconstruction and Stabilization launched the Civilian Response Corps. This new corps will enable the government to rapidly deploy civilian experts with the right skills to trouble spots around the world, and it has several key components.

First, the Civilian Response Corps has an active component made up of civilian experts from many government agencies that are available for full-time deployment to at-risk countries. This corps will eventually include 250 personnel from the Departments of State, Justice, Agriculture, and Commerce, the USAID, and other civilian agencies with relevant expertise. Second, the Civilian Response Corps has a standby component made up of government employees who volunteer to be an on-call supplemental force that can deploy for reconstruction and stabilization missions on short notice. This component will have 500 members by the end of 2009, and will eventually have 2,000 members. Third, the Civilian Response Corps will have a reserve component that functions much like the military reserves. It will be made up of approximately 2,000 American citizens with critical skills – such as police officers, judges, prosecutors, engineers, doctors, and public administrators, who sign up to serve on missions abroad when America needs them.

The Administration also began a major transformation of America's diplomatic force posture across the world. Just as the Defense Department launched a global repositioning of America's military forces from Cold War garrisons, the State Department launched a global repositioning of America's diplomatic assets. Under this plan, begun in 2006, the State Department is moving hundreds of Foreign Service positions from Cold War stations in Europe to emerging areas in Africa, South Asia, East Asia, the Middle East, and elsewhere. The Department also established new "American Presence Posts" in key countries – staffed by a single diplomat who moves into a community where there has traditionally been no American diplomatic presence. And to improve public diplomacy, the Department established Regional Public Diplomacy Centers in Europe and the Middle East. These centers are staffed by skilled diplomats fluent in Arabic and other local languages, who can take America's story directly to the people through regional television.

With these and other steps, the Administration transformed our Nation's diplomatic tools so America can better work with partners across the world to help build and sustain democratic states that respond to the needs of their people.

Fighting the Spread of Weapons of Mass Destruction

A central challenge for the United States is to keep the world's most dangerous weapons out of the hands of the world's most dangerous people. For decades, our country relied primarily on arms control regimes – such as the ABM Treaty, the Nuclear Nonproliferation Treaty, and the Biological Weapons Convention – to stop the spread of these weapons. These tools were designed in a different era, when the danger America faced came primarily from a single Cold War adversary that could be deterred by the threat of retaliation. At the start of the 21st century, America faced a very different danger: the growing number of nations, many hostile to America, that were pursuing nuclear, chemical, and biological weapons and had ties to terrorists. If a rogue nation shared these weapons with a terrorist network, they could attack America with catastrophic results. And because these terrorist networks have no borders to protect or capital to defend, they would not likely be deterred by the prospect of massive retaliation.

To deal with these new dangers, the President made clear after the 9/11 attacks that any nation that harbors or supports terrorists, or shares with them the tools of mass murder, will be held responsible and to account. In December 2007, he approved a new declaratory policy which states: "For many years, it has been the policy of the United States that we reserve the right to respond with overwhelming force to the use of weapons of mass destruction against the United States, our people, our forces, and our friends and allies. Additionally, the United States will hold any state, terrorist group, or other non-state actor fully accountable for supporting or enabling terrorist efforts to obtain or use weapons of mass destruction, whether by facilitating, financing, or providing expertise or safe haven for such efforts."

The President also worked to develop and deploy new defenses to protect the American people from WMD attack. In December 2001, the President announced that the United States was withdrawing from the ABM Treaty. In 2004, the Administration activated an initial limited missile defense system capable of protecting American cities from the threat of ballistic missiles from rogue states.

The Administration also confronted regimes with a history of pursuing and proliferating weapons of mass destruction. When Saddam Hussein deceived international inspectors and refused to comply with more than a dozen United Nations resolutions, the President went to the UN Security Council, which gave Saddam one final chance to disclose and disarm or face serious consequences. Saddam refused. So the United States led an international coalition to remove his Ba'athist regime from power. The Iraq Survey Group later determined that Saddam did not have WMD stockpiles. Saddam chose not to allow inspectors to confirm that fact. Inspectors did confirm that Saddam had preserved the capability to reconstitute his WMD programs when the sanctions regime, which was falling apart before Operation Iraqi Freedom, finally collapsed. The removal of the Iraqi regime, a state sponsor of terror, eliminated this danger, and had a "demonstration effect" for regimes across the world – making clear to all that in an era of terrorism and weapons of mass destruction, America would not wait for dangers to gather.

The overthrow of Saddam Hussein's regime liberated 25 million Iraqis. And it had benefits beyond Iraq's borders. The leader of Libya announced in December 2003 that he was abandoning his country's pursuit of weapons of mass destruction. The Libyan nuclear program – the uranium, the centrifuges, the designs to build bombs, as well as key missile components – was flown to secure storage facilities in the United States. Libya committed to destroy its chemical weapons. Today, Libya is out of the business of pursuing weapons of mass destruction and off the list of state sponsors of terror.

Public disclosure of Libya's weapons of mass destruction programs gave momentum to international efforts to roll up the A.Q. Khan nuclear proliferation network, which had spread sensitive nuclear technology to Libya, Iran, and North Korea. Today, A.Q. Khan's activities have been restricted, and his international network for disseminating nuclear technology has been largely dismantled.

The defeat of Saddam also appeared to have changed the calculation of Iran. According to the U.S. intelligence community, the regime in Tehran had started a nuclear weapons program in the late-1980s, and then halted a key part of that program in 2003. America recognized that the most effective way to persuade Iran not to pursue nuclear weapons and halt its entire effort was to have partners at its side. So the Administration supported international negotiations led by our allies in Europe. This diplomacy yielded an encouraging result, when in late 2003 Iran agreed to suspend its acknowledged uranium enrichment program and allow the IAEA enhanced access to its nuclear related facilities.

In 2006, Iran reversed course and announced it would begin enriching again. In response, America imposed tough financial restrictions, and supported multiple UN resolutions that required member states to prevent transfers of nuclear and missile technology to Iran, as well as restricting travel and freezing assets of Iranian nationals involved in the country's nuclear program. In 2006, the United States announced that it would join talks with Iran if Iran fully and verifiably suspended all enrichment-related and reprocessing activities as the European negotiators and the UN Security Council had demanded. The United States and its partners twice offered Iran diplomatic and economic incentives to suspend enrichment, including promising to support a peaceful civilian nuclear power program. Iran rejected these offers. Since that time, America has continued to pursue diplomacy and rally the world to confront and stop Iran from developing the capability to produce nuclear weapons. The President made America's bottom line clear: "For the safety of our people and the peace of the world, America will not allow Iran to develop a nuclear weapon."

For North Korea, the President established a new multilateral framework known as the Six-Party Talks. When North Korea pulled out of the talks in 2006 and conducted long-range ballistic missile and nuclear weapons tests, the President secured support from China, Russia, and other nations for a UN Security Council Resolution that imposed tough new sanctions on Pyongyang. The sanctions worked, and North Korea came back to the table. As a result, in 2007, North Korea began disabling its plutonium production facilities at Yongbyon. And in 2008, North Korea provided a declaration of its plutonium production capabilities, including a confidential minute addressing its uranium enrichment and proliferation activities. The United States, China, Russia, South Korea, and Japan are together pressing North Korea for a comprehensive verification protocol. While much more work remains to achieve the removal of all nuclear material and weapons from North Korea, the Six-Party process the President established has kept the pressure on Pyongyang. And it has established a new security structure in Northeast Asia that will help future presidents handle other security challenges in the region.

As the President confronted regimes pursuing and proliferating weapons of mass destruction, he created new institutions to help stop the spread of these dangerous weapons.

The Administration established the Proliferation Security Initiative, a coalition of more than 90 nations that are working together to stop shipments of weapons of mass destruction, their delivery systems, and related materials on land, at sea, and in the air.

The Administration launched the Container Security Initiative to detect and stop the movement of dangerous materials at foreign ports and intercept these materials before they are placed on vessels destined for the United States. And the Administration created the Megaports Program, which deploys radiation detection equipment at high-volume international seaports and trains local personnel to check for nuclear or other radioactive materials.

The Administration launched the Global Threat Reduction Initiative, which has secured more than 600 vulnerable nuclear sites around the world; helped convert 57 nuclear reactors in 32 countries from highly-enriched uranium to low-enriched uranium; and removed enough material for more than 40 nuclear bombs from around the world.

The Administration created the Global Nuclear Energy Partnership, which is working with 21 nations – including leaders in nuclear energy, like Russia, France, and Japan – to help nations expand civilian nuclear energy while decreasing the risk of nuclear weapons proliferation and addressing the challenge of nuclear waste disposal.

The Administration worked with the G-8 leaders to launch the Global Partnership Against the Spread of Weapons and Materials of Mass Destruction – a $20 billion international effort to destroy chemical weapons, secure and dispose of nuclear and fissile materials, and help former weapons scientists find new lines of work.

The Administration and the Russian Federation launched the Global Initiative to Combat Nuclear Terrorism, a coalition of 75 nations that are using their own resources to stop the illicit spread of nuclear materials. The United States and Russia also launched the Bratislava Initiative to accelerate and expand their bilateral nuclear security cooperation. Under this initiative, nearly 150 Russian sites containing nuclear warheads and hundreds of metric tons of weapons usable material were secured by the end of 2008.

In 2005, the President issued a new Executive Order authorizing the Departments of the Treasury and State to financially target proliferators and their support networks in the same way in which terrorists are targeted financially. And in 2008, the President issued two directives to strengthen export controls over highly sensitive goods and technologies so they do not reach those who aim to do us harm, while at the same time streamlining procedures for the legitimate trade in controlled goods.

These actions established the new strategies, tools, and institutions necessary to confront and work to prevent the proliferation of the world's most dangerous weapons.

★

BUILDING A MORE
HOPEFUL WORLD

President Bush believes that when Americans see suffering, the conscience of our country demands we act to alleviate it. He also believes that our security ultimately depends on changing the conditions that breed the resentment and despair that help terrorists recruit. For both of these reasons, the President worked to spread hope and opportunity to dark corners of the world. His Administration did so through a number of innovative programs that transformed millions of lives in Africa and other developing regions.

The President's Emergency Plan for AIDS Relief

When President Bush took office, a plague was sweeping the continent of Africa – destroying lives, ravaging communities, and stealing the future of entire nations. Millions of people on the continent had HIV, yet in Sub-Saharan Africa, only 50,000 people living with HIV were receiving the antiretroviral treatment they urgently needed.

Four months after taking office, the President announced a founding contribution of $200 million to help launch a new global fund to help counter the spread of AIDS, tuberculosis, and malaria. The following year, in June 2002, the President launched another initiative to combat this terrible disease – a new $500 million effort to prevent mother-to-child transmission of the HIV virus. "This effort," the President said, "will allow us to treat one million women annually, and reduce mother-to-child transmission by 40 percent within five years or less in target countries."

These two initiatives were significant – but the President determined more needed to be done. So in his 2003 State of the Union address, the President announced a landmark initiative – the President's Emergency Plan for AIDS Relief, or PEPFAR. He asked Congress for an unprecedented commitment – $15 billion over five years – to support a comprehensive plan to combat this disease.

Congress responded by passing the "United States Leadership Against Global HIV/AIDS, Malaria, and Tuberculosis Act of 2003" with overwhelming bipartisan support. The President signed the bill in May 2003 – formally launching the largest initiative in human history by any country to fight a single disease.

Since then, PEPFAR has helped bring life-saving treatment to more than 2.1 million people around the world; supported prevention of mother-to-child HIV transmission during more than 16 million pregnancies; prevented an estimated 240,000 infant infections; provided care for more than 10 million people worldwide, including more than four million orphans and vulnerable children; and supported more than 57 million counseling and testing sessions for men, women, and children.

The President and Mrs. Bush saw the effects of the Emergency Plan in February of 2008, when they traveled to Benin, Tanzania, Rwanda, Ghana, and Liberia. They visited clinics funded through PEPFAR and met children whose lives had been saved because of the good hearts of the American people. Thousands of people lined the roadsides during their visit, cheering and waving American flags in gratitude.

With PEPFAR a clear success, the President asked Congress in May of 2007 to reauthorize PEPFAR and double America's historic commitment to fight HIV/AIDS. The following year, Congress passed and the President signed PEPFAR reauthorization legislation, committing the United States - and $50 billion - to the fight over the next five years.

Malaria Initiative

The President also led the fight to confront another disease on the continent of Africa – malaria. In 2004, approximately a million Africans were dying each year of malaria, and the vast majority of them were children under five – their lives ended by nothing more than a mosquito bite.

So in 2005, the President announced an initiative to increase dramatically America's commitment to fighting malaria in Africa. He set an historic goal – to cut the number of malaria-related deaths in half. And to meet this goal, he committed the United States to spend $1.2 billion over five years to provide bed nets, indoor spraying, and anti-malaria medicine in 15 African countries. In the three years since it was launched, this Initiative has provided malaria treatment and prevention services to more than 25 million people in 15 targeted countries.

The President also supported the fight against malaria through the Global Fund to Fight AIDS, Tuberculosis, and Malaria. Approximately one quarter of the $3.3 billion the United States has contributed to the Global Fund has been used for anti-malaria projects.

And to ensure the United States remains committed to the fight against Malaria, the PEPFAR reauthorization bill also authorizes an additional $5 billion for the Malaria Initiative.

For many illnesses, there is no known relief. For malaria, we know exactly what it takes to prevent and treat the disease. All that is required is the will to act. Because Americans have shown that will, many lives are being saved in Africa and beyond.

Neglected Tropical Diseases

As the success of PEPFAR and the Malaria Initiative transformed lives across the world, President Bush saw another opportunity to spread healing to impoverished communities by taking on the challenge of neglected tropical diseases like river blindness and hook worm.

In 2006, the Bush Administration launched a $100 million program through USAID called the Neglected Tropical Diseases Control Project. Under this project, the Administration would use donated or discounted drugs to deliver treatment to 40 million people over five years – focusing on five African countries. The program became fully operational in 2007, and in its first year reached 14 million people in Burkina Faso, Ghana, Mali, Niger, and Uganda.

In February 2008, President Bush traveled to Africa. In Ghana, he announced that the Administration was expanding the program – providing $350 million to reach more than 300 million people in Africa, Asia, and Latin America over five years. A few months later, in July 2008, the President traveled to Japan for the G-8 Summit, where he challenged America's G-8 partners, foundations, and private donors to join the effort to fight neglected tropical diseases. G-8 Leaders agreed to work to help reach at least 75 percent of people affected by these diseases around the world. In September 2008, the British government became the first of America's G-8 partners to back this pledge, when they announced an approximately $75 million commitment to fight neglected tropical diseases. As more nations follow through, this initiative will reach more people in the developing world – and bring hope and healing to desperate communities across the globe.

Expanding and Transforming Development Assistance

When the President took office, he found America's development assistance efforts did too little to promote liberty, democracy, and good governance. Success was measured by the amount of money delivered, rather than the measurable change it brought about. And funding for America's foreign assistance efforts was in decline.

In March 2002, the President attended a United Nations development conference in Monterrey, Mexico, where he announced a plan to increase U.S. foreign aid and transform the way aid is delivered. He proposed a 50 percent increase in core U.S. development assistance by 2006. And he announced a revolutionary initiative called the Millennium Challenge Account. Under this initiative, the United States would provide aid only to nations that govern justly, invest in their people, and make political and economic reforms.

By 2007, American development assistance had reached $21.8 billion, more than double the 2000 level. And in January 2004, the Administration established the Millennium Challenge Corporation, or MCC, to administer the Millennium Challenge Account. Through September 2008, the MCC had committed more than $6.3 billion in assistance in compacts with 18 countries that have met rigorous, objective, and transparent eligibility requirements. The MCC, in partnership with the U.S. Agency for International Development, has also committed more than $400 million for "threshold" programs in another 19 countries – helping their governments improve specific policies in order to qualify for formal compacts.

In all, MCC programs have invested $6.7 billion in 35 countries around the world. And these investments are yielding benefits far beyond the projects they fund. For example, the MCC has provided a significant financial incentive for governments to expand political liberty, economic freedom, and the rule of law – making our development efforts a vital tool in support of the President's freedom agenda. And countries that win MCC grants are attracting additional private-sector investment because they have been identified by the U.S. government as good places to do business.

Recognizing that the key to a prosperous future is education, in July 2001, President Bush launched the Africa Education Initiative. By 2010, this program will have trained more than 920,000 teachers, distributed 15 million textbooks and learning materials, and provided more than 550,000 scholarships primarily to help girls go to school. To build on this progress, in 2007 the President announced a new $525 million initiative to improve education in Ethiopia, Ghana, Honduras, Liberia, Mali, and Yemen. In 2007, he also launched the Partnership for Latin American Youth to provide English language and vocational training to disadvantage youth. With these and other education programs, the Bush Administration has helped children in Africa and Latin America become the future doctors, lawyers, engineers, and entrepreneurs vital to the developing world's future.

The President also made the private sector a key partner in development. In all, the Administration leveraged a combined total of $9 billion in public and private resources through 680 partnerships with more than 1,700 organizations. For every dollar in U.S. assistance, the private sector has contributed three dollars.

Finally, the President reformed U.S. aid programs to more closely align them with U.S. foreign policy goals. He elevated development by including it as a pillar of America's 2002 National Security Strategy, which declared that development is "one of the top priorities of U.S. policy." The President created the new position of Director of Foreign Assistance at the Department of State to oversee all assistance programs and make certain American aid is being used to advance America's objectives in the world.

During his eight years in office, President Bush set in motion the largest transformation of U.S. assistance efforts in nearly five decades. The programs he established, and the innovative ways he carried them out, have helped change millions of lives across the world. And they have advanced the cause of peace in the world, and the security of the United States.

Debt Relief

When the President took office, one of the greatest challenges facing many developing nations was the crushing burden of debt. In 2005, the President, together with U.K. Prime Minister Tony Blair, led the effort at the Gleneagles G-8 Summit to create the Multilateral Debt Relief Initiative, or MDRI. The initiative called for 100 percent cancellation of eligible debt obligations to the World Bank, the African Development Bank, and the International Monetary Fund. With the additional debt relief provided by the Inter-American Development Bank, MDRI has eliminated more than $42 billion in current and future multilateral debt service for 25 countries in Africa and other parts of the developing world. The President also supported efforts with other creditors to cancel additional debt through the Enhanced Heavily Indebted Poor Countries (HIPC) Initiative. Taken together, MDRI and the enhanced HIPC initiative will eventually remove a debt burden of more than $110 billion in current and future debt service for 34 heavily indebted poor countries.

The Administration encouraged the World Bank, the IMF, and other multilateral development banks to provide increased levels of assistance through grants instead of loans. Today, thanks to the Administration's leadership, the World Bank's International Development Association has substantially increased the share of its assistance to poorest nations in grants, not loans. And since 2002, the United States has made commitments of $1.23 billion to the African Development Fund – which is also increasing its share of grants for the poorest nations, in place of loans.

Humanitarian Aid

Under President Bush's leadership, the United States continues to be the largest provider of food assistance in the world. Since 2002, the Administration provided $16 billion in food assistance – helping ensure that more than 300 million people around the world do not go hungry. When a global food crisis struck late in the President's second term, the Bush Administration announced it would provide more than $5.5 billion to address global hunger in 2008 and 2009. And to help countries become more self-sufficient, the United States supplied poor farmers across the developing world with fertilizer and water-management systems; distributed better seeds to boost yields; and worked with partner nations to improve water-management systems.

During the President's time in office, the United States came to the aid of victims of devastating earthquakes in Pakistan, India, and Iran. When a massive tsunami struck Asian countries in 2004, killing more than 229,000 people, the President responded with urgency and compassion – dispatching military aid and humanitarian assistance to devastated communities, and rallying nations in the Asia Pacific in a massive relief effort. In 2008, when Cyclone Nargis struck the nation of Burma, the United States delivered aid to the victims of this terrible disaster.

In all these ways, the Bush Administration showed that Americans care deeply about the human condition and stand ready to act when we see suffering in faraway lands.

Human Trafficking

When the President took office, he found a new form of slavery on the rise. Between 600,000 and 800,000 human beings were being trafficked across international borders each year. Of these, it is believed that 80 percent were women and girls and two-thirds were forced into sexual servitude. According to the United Nations, the trafficking in human beings had become the third largest source of money for organized crime, after arms and drugs. Here in the United States, many victims were being trafficked across our borders each year.

In 2003, at the United Nations, the President called on governments to pass laws making such abuse a crime. Since then, nations across the world have passed more than 150 new acts, more than 32,000 traffickers have been prosecuted worldwide, and nearly 17,000 have been convicted. To support this global effort, the Administration provided more than $528 million to support anti-trafficking programs benefitting more than 120 countries. The Administration also released an annual "Trafficking in Persons Report" detailing the record of every nation in the fight against human trafficking – speeding action by dozens of nations hoping to avoid sanctions. And in 2004, the United States created a "Special Watch List" of problem countries that require special scrutiny.

Here at home, the Department of Justice opened more than 1,000 new trafficking investigations. Since 2001, the Department of Justice has secured convictions of more than 500 traffickers. The Administration also rallied the armies of compassion in our society to help – providing $35 million in grants to local groups that are helping those who have suffered at the hands of traffickers. The Justice Department provided $5.5 million to organizations providing shelters and other services for trafficking victims. The Administration provided more than 2,400 special visas, called "T-Visas," that allow trafficking victims and their family members to remain in the United States and receive the same services and counseling that are provided to refugees.

The Administration also cracked down on American citizens who abuse innocent children abroad. In 2003, President Bush signed the PROTECT Act, which allows U.S. law enforcement to prosecute Americans who travel abroad and engage in sex with minors without having to prove prior intent, expands the statute of limitations, and doubles the maximum sentence for these crimes. Backed by this new law, the Administration launched Operation Predator, a comprehensive effort to protect children from international sex tourists, traffickers, and pornography and prostitution rings. Since 2003, this operation has resulted in more than 11,000 arrests nationwide.

BUILDING A MORE
HOPEFUL AMERICA

Faith-Based and Community Initiative

When President Bush entered office, many nonprofits in communities across America had the desire to help their fellow citizens but lacked the capacity and resources to successfully compete for Federal funds. And because many of these organizations were faith-based, they were often unable to receive support from the Federal Government.

The President set about to change this based on his philosophy of compassionate conservatism. This approach was compassionate because it was rooted in a timeless truth – that we ought to love our neighbors as we would like to be loved ourselves. And this approach was conservative because it recognized that bureaucracies can put money in people's hands, but they cannot put hope in people's hearts.

To implement this new approach, the President used his first Executive Order to establish the Office of Faith Based and Community Initiatives at the White House. During his Administration, he created Faith-Based and Community offices at 11 Federal agencies. The Administration tasked these offices with lowering the legal and institutional barriers that prevented government and faith-based groups from working as partners.

The Administration carried out this mission in two key ways. First, the Administration leveled the playing field for faith-based groups and other charities. The Administration educated religious groups about their rights and responsibilities; made the Federal grant-application process more accessible and transparent; trained Federal employees to ensure that the government does not discriminate against faith-based organizations; created new models for Federal programs that brought grassroots nonprofits into the delivery of services; and implemented regulations to ensure that these groups did not have to give up their religious character to receive taxpayer money.

Second, the Administration advanced policies to enable greater support for faith-based and other community groups. Working with Congress, the President amended the tax code to provide greater incentives for charitable donations. He also established the Compassion Capital Fund to increase the effectiveness and impact of faith-based and community groups serving the needy.

The Administration upheld its promise to treat community and faith-based organizations as trusted partners. And the results have been impressive. For example, through their partnerships with the government, faith-based and community organizations have helped match more than 100,000 children of prisoners with adult mentors and have helped more than 260,000 addicts along the path toward clean lives. And they have been vital partners in the President's efforts to combat suffering and disease across the world from human trafficking to HIV/AIDS.

Thirty-six governors established their own Faith-Based and Community Initiatives offices or liaisons. More than 70 mayors have similar programs at the municipal level, and over the past eight years, the Initiative has trained more than 150,000 social entrepreneurs. The Faith-Based and Community Initiative will continue transforming lives long after the President leaves office.

USA Freedom Corps

Following the 9/11 attacks, Americans responded with characteristic grace and generosity – donating time and money to help our Nation recover. Millions were eager to find ways to contribute to their fellow citizens. To tap into that spirit, President Bush used his 2002 State of the Union address to issue a call for every American to "commit at least two years, 4,000 hours over the rest of your lifetime, to the service of your neighbors and your Nation." And he launched USA Freedom Corps – a new office at the White House to develop national and community service policy and programs, connect people with opportunities to serve, and foster a culture of citizenship, responsibility, and service.

As part of USA Freedom Corps, the President created Citizen Corps – a new program to engage local officials, law enforcement, and volunteers to ensure communities across our Nation are ready to respond to future disasters. Today, there are nearly one million Citizen Corps volunteers serving in more than 2,000 communities nationwide.

In 2003, the President also created a new program called Volunteers for Prosperity, which matches skilled American professionals with service opportunities in the developing world. Since its creation, Volunteers for Prosperity has helped deploy approximately 116,000 talented Americans to support initiatives such as the President's Emergency Plan for AIDS Relief and the President's Malaria Initiative.

USA Freedom Corps also expanded existing national service programs such as the Peace Corps and AmeriCorps. Under the President's leadership, the Peace Corps has now grown to nearly 8,000 volunteers throughout the world, a 37-year high. And today, more than 74,000 people serve their fellow citizens through AmeriCorps each year.

USA Freedom Corps also fostered a culture of service by encouraging the private sector to step forward. For example, through the "A Billion and Change" program, the Administration has encouraged corporate professionals to donate their services to charities and non-profits. This initiative has already garnered partnership commitments from more than 150 top corporate leaders across the country.

To encourage more Americans to serve, USA Freedom Corps launched a website – volunteer.gov – which is the largest clearinghouse of volunteer opportunities in America. The database is searchable by ZIP code so Americans can find opportunities in their own communities. The President also launched a volunteer recognition program through which he personally met and honored nearly 700 volunteers during his domestic travel across the country. The President created the President's Council on Service and Civic Participation and the President's Volunteer Service Award, which has now been given to more than 1.4 million Americans.

In 2002, the Administration became the first to conduct a regular survey of volunteerism through the U.S. Census Bureau. In 2007, this survey found that nearly 61 million Americans now volunteer their time to help their neighbors.

ECONOMY & BUDGET

When President Bush took office in January 2001, he inherited a recession and an economy struggling under a high tax burden. Then came the attacks of September 11, 2001, which caused immense economic damage, and the revelation of a series of corporate scandals that shook confidence in the economy. Together, all these events contributed to the loss of 2.7 million jobs between February 2001 and August 2003, and three straight years of falling Federal tax revenues.

The President worked with Congress to pass historic tax relief to get the economy moving again.

2001 and 2003 Tax Relief

During his 2000 campaign, President Bush put forward a proposal for broad-based tax relief that would: replace the five tax rate structure of 15 percent, 28 percent, 31 percent, 36 percent, and 39.6 percent with four, lower rates of 10 percent, 15 percent, 25 percent, and 33 percent; double the child tax credit to $1,000 per child; substantially reduce the marriage penalty; eliminate the death tax; allow taxpayers who do not itemize to deduct charitable contributions; increase the annual contribution limit on Educational Savings Accounts from $500 to $5,000, and expand them beyond college, down to kindergarten; and eliminate the Social Security earnings test – an unfair burden on working retirees.

In February 2001, he put forward the same tax relief plan he had unveiled on the campaign trail. In June 2001, Congress approved a tax relief package that included all of the President's proposals, with some additional proposals from Congress, including a Senate plan to provide the reduction in the 15 percent tax rate as a rebate check. These rebates were designed to stimulate consumption by providing $300 of tax relief to each individual taxpayer through a direct check. The President signed the tax relief bill into law on June 7, 2001.

Soon after the 2002 mid-term elections, President Bush proposed a new tax relief package to accelerate the rate reductions in the 2001 bill and reduce capital taxation by ending the double taxation of dividends. The President outlined his plan in a speech in January 2003, where he made a new argument for cutting the top income tax rate. He explained that since approximately 30 million Americans include small business income when they file their individual tax returns, a cut in the top rate is a tax cut for small businesses. Less than five months after the President's speech, Congress passed legislation to enact the second round of the Bush tax cuts. The President signed the bill into law on May 28, 2003. By August of 2003, the economy was expanding and creating jobs again.

The President's tax cuts reduced taxes for every American who pays income taxes and eliminated income taxes entirely for 13 million low-income Americans. By the end of 2008, the President's tax relief allowed the American people to keep $1.7 trillion of their own money. The pro-growth policies and tax relief helped produce six years of uninterrupted economic growth, and a record 52 straight months of job creation that produced more than eight million new jobs. From 2000 to 2007, real GDP grew by more than 17 percent, a remarkable gain of nearly $2.1 trillion. This growth was driven in part by increased labor productivity gains that have averaged 2.5 percent annually since 2001, a rate that exceeds the averages of the 1970s, 1980s, and 1990s. In the same period, real after-tax income per capita increased by more than 11 percent, and there was a 4.7 percent increase in the number of new businesses formed. The President followed a clear principle: allowing people to keep more of their money is the best way to help our economy grow.

2008 Stimulus Package

In late 2007, the President grew increasingly concerned about an economic slowdown and proposed an economic stimulus plan. In January 2008, he gave a speech laying out the principles on which such a stimulus should be based: "This growth package must be big enough to make a difference in an economy as large and dynamic as ours – which means it should be about one percent of GDP. This growth package must be built on broad-based tax relief that will directly affect economic growth – and not the kind of spending that would have little immediate impact on our economy. This growth package must be temporary and take effect right away – so we can get help to our economy when it needs it most. And this growth package must not include any tax increases."

On February 13, less than a month after calling on Congress to act, the President signed into law the Economic Stimulus Act of 2008. The bill provided temporary tax incentives for businesses to make investments in their companies and create jobs, and it provided tax relief in the form of tax rebates of up to $600 for individuals and $1,200 for married couples, with additional rebates for families with children. In all, the final bill provided needed tax relief to more than 100 million American households.

In the months that followed, other shocks weakened the economy. Financial markets were hit hard in the spring by the collapse of a Wall Street firm. A continued deterioration in the housing market was followed by skyrocketing food and energy prices, and troubles at Fannie Mae and Freddie Mac exposed further weaknesses in credit markets and financial institutions. Despite these shocks, the economy grew at 2.8 percent in the 2nd quarter.

2008 Financial Crisis

Then a financial crisis struck, and America saw dramatic swings in the stock market and a string of failures and near-failures of major financial institutions. By mid-September, the global financial system seized up. Banks restricted lending to each other. Credit markets began to freeze. Businesses found it harder to borrow money. The system was on the verge of collapse. It became clear that emergency legislation was needed to allow the Treasury Department and the Federal Reserve to intervene, stabilize the financial system, and minimize further damage to the economy.

On September 24, 2008, President Bush addressed the Nation from the White House. He explained that over the past decade, the world had experienced a period of strong economic growth. Nations accumulated huge amounts of savings and looked for safe places to invest them. Because of our attractive political, legal, and entrepreneurial climates, the United States and other developed nations received a large share of that money. The massive inflow of foreign capital, combined with low interest rates, produced a period of easy credit, which affected our economy, particularly the housing market. Flush with cash, many lenders issued mortgages that many borrowers could not afford. Financial institutions then purchased these loans, packaged them together, and converted them into complex securities designed to yield large returns. These securities were then purchased by investors and financial institutions in the United States and around the world, often with little analysis of their true underlying value.

The financial crisis was ignited when booming housing markets began to decline. As home values dropped, many borrowers defaulted on their mortgages, and institutions holding securities backed by those mortgages suffered serious losses. When capital ran short, many financial institutions in America and Europe faced severe financial jeopardy. This led to high-profile failures of financial institutions, which contributed to sharp declines in the equity markets.

With the situation becoming more precarious by the day, the President told the American people that he faced a choice: to step in with dramatic government action or to stand back and allow the rapidly developing crisis to jeopardize the financial security of all. The President chose to act. The Administration asked Congress to approve a plan for the Federal Government to help banks to resume lending to American families and businesses, and help our economy grow. The Administration also took action to shore up money market funds that were in danger of collapsing by offering insurance to boost investor confidence.

On September 29, the House of Representatives rejected the financial rescue plan by a margin of 228-205. Chastened by the negative stock market reaction to the House vote, negotiators went back to the table. They added a new provision to the bill temporarily expanding Federal insurance for bank and credit union deposits from $100,000 to $250,000 – a safeguard for consumers and small businesses. The Senate approved the revised bill, and on October 3, the House approved the Emergency Economic Stabilization Act of 2008. President Bush signed the bill into law within hours of passage.

The new law created a mechanism called the Troubled Asset Relief Program and a new government insurance program to guarantee the value of others. The legislation gave the Treasury Department flexibility in how it designs and implements these programs.

By the time the legislation had passed, however, economic conditions had worsened considerably. In the two weeks that Congress worked on the bill, the stock market suffered tremendous losses. The global financial crisis had spread well beyond mortgage-related assets, becoming so severe that powerful steps were needed to quickly stabilize the financial system and get credit flowing again. Secretary Paulson and Federal Reserve Chairman Bernanke determined that a program to purchase illiquid mortgages and mortgage-related securities might not be effective or quick enough, and they began considering purchasing equity directly from financial institutions as the fastest and most efficient way to stabilize the financial system.

On October 14, the Treasury Department used the authorities granted by Congress to launch a $250 billion Capital Purchase Program (CPP). By October 28, Treasury had invested Federal funds in eight of the largest U.S. financial institutions. In the weeks that followed, dozens of additional applications were approved and investments made. This rapid infusion of capital enabled banks to absorb losses, as they wrote down or sold troubled assets. And this infusion of capital enabled these banks to increase lending. The same day that the CPP was announced, the Federal Reserve announced a program to support the commercial paper market, and the FDIC put in place a temporary guarantee of certain debt issued by banks.

With these steps, the Federal Government significantly increased investor and public confidence in the banks, helping to stabilize the financial system and prevent a systemic collapse. By addressing the problems proactively, and being flexible enough to change strategy, the Administration prevented a far worse financial crisis.

As the tumultuous year in financial markets neared an end, America's auto manufacturers also neared failure, presenting the President with a difficult choice. Some firms warned the Administration and Congress that they were unable to borrow from private debt markets, and that they were unprepared for an orderly Chapter 11 bankruptcy filing. If they did not receive government loans, a disorderly bankruptcy and liquidation of two of the three large U.S. auto manufacturers looked certain, which would have cost an already weak economy more than a million additional jobs.

Congress had already appropriated funds to subsidize loans to auto manufacturers, but they were limited to paying for upgrades to produce more fuel-efficient vehicles. The Administration proposed legislation to redirect these funds to provide more generalized loans, but Congress failed to act. In late December, the President faced a choice: to use some of the funds previously appropriated to stabilize the financial system to provide loans to American auto manufacturers or to allow them to go bankrupt with an economy already in recession and during a transition to a new President. As he said: "This is a difficult situation that involves fundamental questions about the proper role of government. On the one hand, government has a responsibility not to undermine the private enterprise system. On the other hand, government has a responsibility to safeguard the broader health and stability of our economy."

The President chose to act. He authorized loans from the Treasury funds to U.S. auto manufacturers, but with conditions that any firm taking a loan had months to become viable, defined as the firm having a positive net present value. If the firm was not viable by that date, it must repay the loan and, presumably, file for bankruptcy.

The Housing Crisis

A root cause of the economic downturn was related to the decline of the housing market, and the Administration took early actions to help homeowners avoid preventable foreclosures. In September 2007, the Federal Housing Administration (FHA) launched a new program called FHASecure that gave the FHA greater flexibility to help distressed homeowners refinance their homes. The following month, the Administration helped facilitate the creation of the HOPE NOW Alliance – a voluntary effort by mortgage lenders, investors, and counselors to help struggling homeowners to refinance or modify their mortgages. By the end of 2008, HOPE NOW and FHASecure had together helped more than two million individuals and families.

The most important step the Administration took to stabilize the housing market came in September 2008, when it acted to prevent the failure of Fannie Mae and Freddie Mac. These two government sponsored enterprises (GSEs) owned or securitized trillions in mortgage debt, and their failure would have threatened the entire financial system.

The Administration had warned of the risks posed by Fannie Mae and Freddie Mac since 2001. Beginning in 2003, the Administration put forward proposals to reform Fannie Mae and Freddie Mac and reduce their risks. Unfortunately, these warnings went unheeded by Congress. But by the summer of 2008, it became clear that emergency legislation was needed to reform them and prevent them from failing. On July 30, the President signed the Housing and Economic Recovery Act of 2008, which gave the Treasury Department the authority to use tax-payer dollars to backstop Fannie Mae and Freddie Mac. And it created a new regulator to oversee these institutions called the Federal Housing Finance Agency.

Following passage of the emergency housing legislation, it became clear that these GSEs needed to be reorganized. So on September 7, the new regulator placed Fannie Mae and Freddie Mac into conservatorship and replaced both of their CEOs, and the Treasury Department put in place a preferred stock purchase agreement.

As a result of these actions, Fannie Mae and Freddie Mac are operating on a more stable footing, although the risks they pose have not been eliminated. By stabilizing both these enterprises, the Administration enabled them to continue making mortgage finance available and affordable, so our economy can work through the stress in the housing market.

International Summit

The Administration also acted quickly with our international partners to stabilize the global financial system. In November 2008, the President hosted a summit in Washington on financial markets and the world economy. Leaders from developed and developing nations that account for nearly 90 percent of the world economy attended, along with representatives of the World Bank, the International Monetary Fund (IMF), the United Nations, and the Financial Stability Forum.

The gathered leaders agreed on several principles and actions. They agreed to make financial markets more transparent and accountable so that investors around the world can understand the true value of the assets they purchase; to ensure that all markets, firms, and financial products are subject to proper regulation or oversight; to work to enhance the integrity of their financial markets; to strengthen cooperation among the world's financial authorities; and to reform international financial institutions such as the IMF and the World Bank.

The declaration, agreed to by all the leaders at the summit, stated: "We recognize that these reforms will only be successful if grounded in a commitment to free market principles, including the rule of law, respect for private property, open trade and investment, competitive markets, and efficient, effectively regulated financial systems. These principles are essential to economic growth and prosperity and have lifted millions out of poverty, and have significantly raised the global standard of living."

In a speech in New York City before the summit, the President expanded on this theme, making clear that while the crisis threatened free economies, the cause of the problems we faced was not free market capitalism. He said, "the crisis was not a failure of the free market system. And the answer is not to try to reinvent that system. It is to fix the problems we face, make the reforms we need, and move forward with the free market principles that have delivered prosperity and hope to people across the globe."

Faced with the worst financial crisis in a generation, the President acted boldly. He took unprecedented steps to recapitalize financial institutions and prevent the disorderly collapse of large, interconnected enterprises. In September 2008, the American economy had been at a tipping point – with credit markets largely frozen and financial institutions, businesses, and consumers left without the funding and credit necessary to keep our economy going. By January 2009, credit markets were beginning to thaw; interbank lending rates had come down; businesses were gaining access to essential short-term financing; a measure of stability was returning to financial systems around the world; and the government had the tools, resources, and authorities in place to deal with the financial crisis.

Discretionary Spending and Earmark Reform

During his time in office, the President set a clear principle to guide the Federal Government's spending decisions: "The American people," he said, "expect us to spend their tax dollars wisely, or not at all."

The President increased discretionary spending for defense and homeland security to keep America safe. At the same time, he reduced the growth rate of non-security discretionary spending, bringing it below the rate of inflation. When the President took office, this spending was growing at a rate of 16 percent. By 2005, the President had reduced its growth to just two percent. He maintained that fiscal discipline in the years that followed.

The President confronted Congress over earmarks. From his first days in office, he urged Congress to approve legislative line-item veto authority that would allow him to strip wasteful earmarks out of spending bills. In 2006, the Administration succeeded in securing House passage of a line-item veto bill, as well as committee approval in the Senate. But the full Senate failed to act.

Meanwhile, the number and cost of earmarks continued to grow. In 1991, appropriations bills approved by Congress contained 546 earmarks that cost taxpayers approximately $3 billion. By 2001, the number had grown to 6,333 earmarks and the cost to taxpayers had increased to more than $18 billion. And despite his efforts to reduce this practice, by the start of his second term in 2005, the cost of these earmarks had increased slightly to nearly $19 billion, while the number had ballooned to 13,497. In his 2007 State of the Union address, the President challenged Congress to enact meaningful earmark reform. He said: "These special interest items are often slipped into bills at the last hour – when not even C-SPAN is watching.... Over 90 percent of earmarks never make it to the floor of the House and Senate – they are dropped into Committee reports that are not even part of the bill that arrives on my desk. You did not vote them into law. I did not sign them into law. Yet they are treated as if they have the force of law. The time has come to end this practice."

To help shine a spotlight on these earmarks, the President created a new website – www.earmarks.gov. The final earmark totals for the 2008 appropriations bills were less than the 2005 baseline: a 15 percent reduction in number and 13 percent reduction in dollar amount.

In his 2008 State of the Union, the President took the next step, telling Congress: "if you send me an appropriations bill that does not cut the number and cost of earmarks in half, I will send it back to you with my veto. And tomorrow, I will issue an Executive Order that directs Federal agencies to ignore any future earmark that is not voted on by Congress."

Congress responded to the President's threat to veto earmark-laden spending bills by virtually abandoning its appropriations responsibilities, and passed a five-month continuing resolution that included three regular spending bills, with more than 2,400 new earmarks, and carried over the funding levels from the previous year's appropriations bills, including funding for the earmarks they contained. But because of the President's Executive Order, agencies and departments were barred from funding those old earmarks if they were not voted on by Congress, effectively stripping them from these spending bills.

In his final year in office, the President achieved a more than a 40 percent reduction in the number of earmarks and a nearly 40 percent reduction in the dollar amount. And the President established earmark reform as a top priority for the Nation.

The Deficit

By January 2001, the budget surpluses of the 1990s were already disappearing. The recession the President inherited, followed by the economic shocks and terrorist attacks of 2001 and the costs of waging the war on terror eliminated those surpluses. The 2001 budget had been projected to show a surplus of $184 billion. By 2002, the country faced a deficit of $158 billion, and by 2004, the deficit reached $413 billion, or 3.6 percent of GDP.

As the President's pro-growth policies helped get the economy moving again, tax revenues rebounded. Combined with spending discipline, this allowed the Bush Administration to begin reducing the deficit. In 2004, the President set a goal of cutting the deficit in half in five years. Even with the added costs of Hurricane Katrina and the continuing costs of war, he achieved that goal three years early. In 2006, the deficit fell to $248 billion, or 1.9 percent of GDP.

In 2007 the deficit fell to $162 billion. Unfortunately, the economic slowdown in early 2008 and the $150 billion bipartisan stimulus package Congress passed caused the deficit to rise in 2008. The 2008 financial crisis caused the deficit to rise even further, and the financial rescue package enacted in the fall of 2008 could eventually increase the deficit by as much as $700 billion. However, this $700 billion is an artificial increase since many economists believe that most of the costs of the rescue plan will one day be recovered as the assets the government purchases are eventually sold.

Even so, the size of the 2009 deficit will grow significantly. But the costs that would have arisen if our government had not taken bold action to rescue the economy would have been far greater. As the economy recovers, revenues will begin growing again, mandatory spending will return to normal levels, and much of the cost of the financial rescue plan will be recouped.

Reforming Government

The Bush Administration saved billions of taxpayer dollars by holding agencies accountable for implementing sound management practices. When he took office, President Bush launched the President's Management Agenda, which has caused improper government payments to be reduced by $8 billion since 2004; underutilized real property to be reduced by $8 billion since 2004; and the cost of commercial services by to be reduced by more than an estimated $1 billion per year.

The reforms the President and Federal employees implemented have increased the accountability, transparency, and effectiveness of the Federal Government. All Federal programs and reform efforts now have clear, quantifiable outcome and efficiency goals, and performance ratings; Federal earmarks, contracts, grants, and loans are required to be readily transparent to the general public; all employees are rated on their performance relative to their goals, and salary increases for all Senior Executives and nearly 350,000 career Federal employees are based on their performance; agencies account for their expenditures throughout the year instead of waiting until the end of the year; and there are a series of websites to make it easier for citizens to access Federal benefits and services, including sites that help people file tax returns, apply for Federal jobs and grants, and plan vacations at national parks.

American Competitiveness Initiative

The Administration also worked to strengthen America's ability to compete in the global economy. The President announced a proposal called the American Competitiveness Initiative in his 2006 State of the Union address, saying: "To keep America competitive ... we must continue to lead the world in human talent and creativity. Our greatest advantage in the world has always been our educated, hard-working, ambitious people – and we are going to keep that edge."

Central elements of his proposal were:

- Doubling the Federal commitment to the most critical basic research programs in the physical sciences over ten years.

- Making permanent the research and development tax credit – an $86 billion commitment to encourage bolder private-sector investment in technology.

- Encouraging children to take more math and science classes and making sure those courses are rigorous enough. He proposed training 70,000 high school teachers to lead advanced-placement courses in math and science; creating an Adjunct Teacher Corps to bring 30,000 math and science professionals to teach in our Nation's classrooms over eight years; and providing early help to students who struggle with math.

On August 9, 2007, the President signed the America Competes Act, authorizing major elements of the American Competitiveness Initiative through 2010. Unfortunately, Congress failed to make permanent the R&D tax credit and failed to fund many critical math and science education programs the President requested and Congress had authorized. Still, overall Federal research and development funding increased 57 percent since 2001. And the President secured bipartisan

Congressional approval for a strategy to keep America competitive in the decades to come.

Trade & Investment

When the President took office in 2001, America had free trade agreements in force with just three nations – Israel, Canada, and Mexico. As he prepares to leave office, America has agreements in force with 16 nations. The President's commitment to free trade helped strengthen our economy in a time of challenge, and created opportunities for American businesses across the world.

The President worked to expand trade in the Asia-Pacific region. In 2003, he secured Congressional approval for a free trade agreement with Singapore. The following year, he secured Congressional approval for a free trade agreement with Australia. In 2007, the Administration signed a free trade agreement with South Korea, which the Congress has not yet approved, that is estimated to add more than $10 billion to our economy annually. In 2007, trade in goods between the United States and the nations of the Asia- Pacific region reached $1 trillion. Today, more trade crosses the Pacific than the Atlantic. To expand this trade even further, the United States announced in 2008 that it would participate with Brunei, Chile, New Zealand, Singapore, Australia, Peru, and Vietnam in the negotiation of a Trans-Pacific Strategic Economic Partnership Agreement.

The President worked to expand trade within the Western Hemisphere. In 2003, the President secured Congressional approval of a new free trade agreement with Chile. In 2005, the President worked with Congress to secure approval for the Dominican Republic-Central America Free Trade Agreement. In 2007, the President secured Congressional approval of a free trade agreement between the United States and Peru that is expected to go into effect in 2009. In 2006, the Administration signed a free trade agreement with Colombia, and the following year the Administration signed an agreement with Panama. Congress has yet to approve these two agreements. Nevertheless, overall trade between the United States and the nations of the Western Hemisphere has grown by 84 percent since 2001.

The President worked to expand trade with Sub-Saharan Africa. He signed three separate enhancements of the African Growth and Opportunity Act. The United States also provided $1.6 billion in trade capacity building assistance to African countries from 2001 to 2007. In part as a result of these efforts, two-way trade between the United States and Sub-Saharan Africa nearly tripled during the President's term in office.

The President worked to expand trade and investment in the broader Middle East and North Africa. In September 2001, the President secured Congressional approval for the United States-Jordan Free Trade Agreement. In July 2004, the President secured Congressional approval for a free trade agreement with Morocco. In December 2005, the President secured Congressional approval for a free trade agreement with Bahrain. The President secured Congressional approval in 2006 for a free trade agreement with Oman, which went into effect on January 1, 2009. All these agreements are opening up new markets for American goods and services in the broader Middle East and strengthening our relations with key nations.

The President also worked to expand trade and investment around the world. When the President took office, no global round of trade negotiations had been initiated in more than 14 years. The President took the lead in convening the Doha Round of multilateral trade negotiations under the World Trade Organization. Unfortunately, a Doha agreement was not concluded during the President's term. But the Administration advanced these talks and laid the groundwork for a successful outcome to the Doha Round.

The free trade agreements brought into force by the Bush Administration opened up markets of an additional 131 million consumers to American goods and services – more than any Administration in history. Overall, American exports increased by 85 percent during the President's time in office. Moreover, American exports to nations with whom the Administration enacted free trade agreements between 2001 and 2008 increased nearly 80 percent faster on average than U.S. exports to the rest of the world.

EDUCATION

When the President took office, too many American children were trapped in schools without challenging academic standards and were shuffled from grade-to-grade because of their age, regardless of their knowledge. The achievement gap between white and minority students was wide – and in some areas it was growing.

President Bush called this "the soft bigotry of low expectations." He was determined to rid our public schools of it. And thanks to the reforms his Administration enacted, student achievement increased, the achievement gap narrowed, and more children are now receiving the education they deserve.

No Child Left Behind

Just three days after his inauguration, the President sent Congress his blueprint for nationwide education reform, which would become the No Child Left Behind Act. The plan emphasized several priorities: in exchange for Federal support, schools would be held accountable for the performance of all their students; student performance would be measured through testing; effective, research-based education programs would be emphasized; flexibility would be increased for States and school districts; and parents would be empowered with more information and more choices. Under the President's plan, academic standards would be set by States, and schools would be held accountable for results. Before the end of his first year in office, Congress passed the No Child Left Behind Act based on these principles and did so with overwhelming bipartisan support.

The Bush Administration quickly set about implementing the new law, and it quickly had a positive impact. Testing showed that the achievement gap between white and African-American students was closing for both fourth- and eighth-graders, and that Hispanic fourth-graders were also narrowing the achievement gap.

In April of 2005, Secretary of Education Margaret Spellings announced new guidelines that gave States incentives to come into full compliance with the law. The guidelines offered greater flexibility to

States that met certain guiding principles of NCLB. Student achievement continued to improve under this new and increased flexibility.

In March 2005, a report from the Council of Great City Schools showed gains in the achievement of urban students, especially in math. And the 2005 Nation's Report Card results revealed that the achievement gap between minority students and white students had shrunk and that progress in fourth grade reading had accelerated dramatically.

In 2007, the President urged Congress to reauthorize and improve the No Child Left Behind Act. Despite the law's encouraging results, Congress failed to do so. But the record of what No Child Left Behind has achieved over the past seven years is clear.

According to the Nation's Report Card, in 2007 fourth and eighth grade math scores were higher than they had ever been. In addition, by the 2007–2008 school year, 48 States and the District of Columbia had either improved or held steady in all academic categories. Nearly one million more students have learned basic math skills since the law was passed.

In terms of closing the achievement gap, African-American and Hispanic students have reached all-time highs in a number of categories. In fourth grade reading, the achievement gap between white and black students is the narrowest it has been since 1992. In math, fourth and eighth grade African-American students achieved their highest scores to date. Hispanic students also posted their highest scores on record in fourth grade reading and in fourth and eighth grade math.

The No Child Left Behind Act's "Reading First" program has also made a big difference for America's students. At the first grade level, 44 States have reported increases in the percentage of students proficient in reading comprehension. Of these, 31 States reported increases of five percentage points or more. And in grade two, 39 States reported improvement – 19 of them by five percentage points or more.

As President Bush leaves office, educators across the country now use data to improve performance. Parents now get report cards to tell them not only how their children are doing, but how their schools are doing. Because of No Child Left Behind, student achievement in America is on the rise and the achievement gap is shrinking.

School Choice

As the President worked to improve our schools, he also acted to offer alternatives to parents of students trapped in struggling public schools that cannot – or will not – improve.

Under the No Child Left Behind Act, parents of any child in a chronically low-performing school can transfer their child to another public school of their choice. The law increased the timeliness and quality of information available to parents about educational options for their children. And the law allowed parents of a low-income child in a struggling school to choose to have their child receive free tutoring.

President Bush's Department of Education also provided unprecedented support for America's public charter schools. Since 2001, more than $1.6 billion has been invested in 1,890 charter schools across America. Since the President took office, the number of charter schools has more than doubled.

The President also worked to expand choice beyond the public school sector. The Administration defended private school choice all the way to the Supreme Court. And in June 2002, the Court declared that private school vouchers were constitutional – freeing the President to pursue legislation that would put scholarship money in the hands of low-income parents with children in failing public schools.

The following year, the President called on Congress to provide scholarships to some of the District of Columbia's poorest children so they could attend the private or parochial school of their choice. In 2004, Congress provided $40 million for education reform in the District, including $14 million for the D.C. Opportunity Scholarship Program. Since 2004, more than 2,600 low income students have received Opportunity Scholarships. Without these scholarships, 86 percent of the participating students would otherwise have remained in failing public schools.

Pell Grants

To put a college education within the reach of more low-income students, the Administration nearly doubled funding for Pell Grants from $8.8 billion when the President took office to $16.2 billion in 2008. The Administration used this increased funding to raise the maximum grant a student could receive from $3,750 in 2001 to more than $4,700 in 2008.

In 2006, the President also secured Congressional approval for legislation to fund two new programs to provide additional rewards to Pell Grant-eligible students who complete more challenging high school coursework and pursue a college major in a subject in high demand in the global economy. These programs are providing $4.5 billion in new funding over five years. In September 2007, the President signed the College Cost Reduction and Access Act, which aims to further increase the maximum grant award by 2012. President Bush's commitment to increasing Pell Grants has helped more than five-and-a-half million students attend college – an increase of nearly 1.2 million since 2001.

Community Colleges & Job Training

In 2004, President Bush announced a new competitive grant program to fund partnerships between community colleges and employers in high-demand job sectors. Through these Community-Based Job Training grants, the Administration has awarded more than $300 million to 211 community colleges across the Nation.

In 2006, President Bush addressed the 2006 graduating class of the Mississippi Gulf Coast Community College, telling them: "The growth and vitality of the Gulf Coast will come from people who open new stores, design new urban plans, create new jobs, teach children, and care for the sick. The key to unlocking these opportunities is knowledge, and millions who want to gain new knowledge come to community colleges just like the one you're graduating from. In the Gulf Coast and beyond, community colleges are the centers of hope and the gateways to social mobility."

Protecting Student Loans

In early 2008, when tightening credit markets threatened the availability of student loans for the 2008-09 school year, the Administration developed an aggressive plan to ensure that students would have uninterrupted access to the Federal aid they needed. The Administration strengthened and readied the Department of Education's Lender-of-Last-Resort program and also increased the capacity of the Direct Loan program. The Administration also worked closely with Congress to pass the Ensuring Continued Access to Student Loans Act. Using the temporary authorities in this law, the Department of Education provided short-term liquidity to lenders through loan purchasing agreements under two new programs – the Loan Purchase program and the Loan Participation program.

As credit markets tightened further in the fall, the Administration worked with Congress to keep these programs in place for the 2009-2010 school year. On October 7, 2008, the President signed a one-year extension of the Ensuring Continued Access to Student Loans Act. Through these and other steps, the Administration worked to ensure that young Americans had access to the loans they need to get a college education.

REDUCING DRUG USE & CRIME

During the President's time in office, major progress was made in reducing drug use by young Americans and reducing the crime that plagued our communities.

Drugs

When President Bush took office, drug use among high school age teens was at near all-time highs. Methamphetamine labs were proliferating, and drugs were flowing into the country at alarming rates. Millions of Americans were in need of drug treatment, but their access to it was hampered by unnecessary restrictions on the organizations that could provide Federally assisted care. And combating drug use had largely fallen off the national agenda.

President Bush was determined to reverse these trends. In February 2002, he released his first National Drug Control Strategy. His strategy had three key elements: 1. reduce demand; 2. interdict supply; and 3. help people who have become addicts get the treatment they need. The Administration has made significant progress on each of these fronts.

In 2002, the President established ambitious goals for reducing illicit drug use: a 10 percent reduction in youth drug use in two years and a 25 percent reduction over five years. To help meet these goals, the Administration doubled funding for the Drug Free Communities Support Program to support community anti-drug coalitions. The Administration also launched a campaign to institute random drug testing in schools across the country. Since 2003, the Department of Education has issued grants that have helped schools implement random testing.

The President also launched an effort to combat the use of anabolic steroids by young people. In his 2004 State of the Union address, the President said: "The use of performance-enhancing drugs like steroids ... sends the wrong message, that there are shortcuts to accomplishment and that performance is more important than character. So tonight I call on team owners, union representatives, coaches, and players to take the lead, to send the right signal, to get tough, and to get rid of steroids now." Major sports leagues have strengthened their policies on steroid use, and in October 2004, the President signed the Anabolic Steroid Control Act, which added additional steroids and steroid precursors to the list of controlled substances.

The Administration worked with law enforcement to uncover and shut down tens of thousands of methamphetamine labs across the country. And in 2006, the President signed the Combat Methamphetamine Epidemic Act, which made it more difficult to obtain precursor chemicals essential for the production of methamphetamine.

The Administration also worked to stop drugs from entering the United States. The Administration worked closely with allies in the Western Hemisphere to fight drug traffickers and seize drugs headed for America. In Colombia, with America's support, President Uribe has put the narco-terrorists on the run. Cocaine production in Colombia dropped by 24 percent between 2001 and 2007, and the flow of export-quality cocaine from Colombia to the United States fell by 54 percent in the same period. In Mexico, President Calderon also stepped forward to defend his country from the drug cartels, and in 2007, President Bush and President Calderon reached an historic agreement in Merida, Mexico, for an intensified joint effort against drug cartels. In June 2008, President Bush signed the Merida Initiative into law, providing an initial $400 million in funding to Mexico and $65 million to countries in Central America and the Caribbean to help combat the drug cartels.

To help Americans break the chains of addiction, the President launched the Access to Recovery program, which provides addicts with vouchers they can redeem at treatment centers of their choice, including faith-based centers. Access to Recovery programs have been established in twenty-two States, the District of Columbia, and five Native American organizations. So far, this program has helped more than 260,000 addicts along the path toward clean lives.

Taken together, the Administration's efforts have yielded measurable results. Illegal drug use by American teens is down by 25 percent – meaning the Administration's efforts have helped approximately 900,000 young people stay clean. Over the past seven years, young people's use of marijuana has dropped by 25 percent; methamphetamine by 50 percent; steroids by 33 percent; hallucinogens by 39 percent; and alcohol by 21 percent.

Crime

The Bush Administration also strengthened America's efforts to combat crime. In May 2001, the President launched Project Safe Neighborhoods, a comprehensive national strategy to vigorously enforce firearm laws and help communities reduce gun crime. He also launched Project Sentry, a Federal-State partnership to improve school safety by prosecuting juveniles who bring guns to school or use them illegally.

In October 2002, the President hosted the first-ever White House Conference on Missing, Exploited, and Runaway Children where he announced steps to strengthen the AMBER Alert program to locate abducted children. The following year, he signed the PROTECT Act, which formally established a National AMBER Alert Coordinator and gave law enforcement valuable new tools to deter, detect, investigate, prosecute, and punish crimes against children.

The President also championed the Keeping Children and Families Safe Act of 2003, which strengthened State and community programs that prevent child abuse and family violence and treat victims of those crimes. Later that year he announced the creation of Family Justice Centers to help local communities provide comprehensive services to victims of domestic violence. The Administration launched Operation Predator, which helped lead to the arrest of more than 11,000 child predators. He signed the Adam Walsh Child Protection and Safety Act in 2006, which expanded the national sex offender registry, strengthened Federal penalties for crimes against children, and required investigators to do background checks on adoptive and foster parents. To deal with the growing problem of identity theft, he signed the Identity Theft Penalty Enhancement Act in July 2004. And the Administration convicted nearly 1,300 individuals of corporate fraud and corruption during the President's term in office.

The President believes that rehabilitation is possible and that a changed life can lead to safer communities. So in 2007, he signed the Second Chance Act, which authorized key elements of the President's successful Prisoner Reentry Initiative to help prisoners effectively reintegrate into the community. The act also enhances drug treatment, monitoring, and transitional services for ex-offenders through partnerships with local corrections agencies and faith-based and community groups.

In December 2008, the Justice Department issued its annual National Crime Victimization Survey. This report found that at the end of the President's second term, rates for every major violent and property crime measured by the survey were at or near the lowest levels recorded since 1973 (the first year that such data was available). The 2007 violent crime rate was 43 percent lower than in 1998, and the rate of property crime declined by 33 percent in the same period. The Bush Administration's policies have helped protect the most vulnerable among us and made our communities safer.

FOSTERING A
CULTURE OF LIFE

President Bush worked to foster a culture of life in our country – speaking up for the humanity of the unborn and taking concrete action to protect innocent life at all its stages.

One of the President's first acts upon taking office was to restore the "Mexico City Policy," which prohibits the U.S. Agency for International Development from awarding family planning grants to any foreign nongovernmental organization that performs abortions or actively promotes abortion as a form of family planning. This policy was first put in place by President Reagan in 1984, but was lifted by President Clinton in 1993. In 2003, President Bush extended the Mexico City Policy to all family planning assistance funded through the Foreign Assistance Act.

The President also worked to secure passage of landmark pro-life legislation. In August 2002, President Bush signed the Born Alive Infants Protection Act, which ensures that every infant born alive – including one who survives an abortion procedure – is considered a person under Federal law. And in April of 2005, the Department of Health and Human Services issued guidance instructing States and hospitals across the country that infants born alive at any stage of development – including after abortion procedures – are protected by the Emergency Medical Treatment and Labor Act and provisions of the Child Abuse Prevention and Treatment Act.

In November 2003, the President signed the Partial Birth Abortion Act, which banned partial birth abortion. The Administration defended this law all the way to the Supreme Court, which upheld the act in 2007. In April 2004, the President signed the Unborn Victims of Violence Act. This law provides that, under Federal law, any person who causes death or injury to a child in the womb will be charged with a separate offense in addition to any charges related to the mother.

The President also worked to expand compassionate support for women struggling with unexpected pregnancies. To encourage adoption, he signed legislation in June 2001, to increase and permanently extended the adoption tax credit. In 2002, he issued a new rule to give

States the option to provide vital health care services to pregnant women and their unborn children who would otherwise be ineligible for coverage under the State Children's Health Insurance Program. In October 2003, he signed legislation to expand Federal support for maternity group homes. In December 2003, he signed the Adoption Promotion Act of 2003, which expanded the adoption incentive payments program. And in November 2007, the United States entered into a treaty designed to ensure that inter-country adoptions are in the best interests of the children.

In 2007, President Bush sent a letter to Congressional leaders warning that he would veto any legislation weakening Federal policies or laws on abortion, encouraging the destruction of human life at any stage, or reversing existing pro-life policies. In 2008, the Administration also took action to protect health care providers' right of conscience, so that they are not forced to participate in an activity to which they object based on their religious beliefs or moral convictions, including performing abortions.

President Bush stood with the pro-life community during his eight years in office, and no President in history has done more in the defense of the unborn.

Stem Cells

In 2001, the President had an important decision to make on the question of embryonic stem cell research. Until that time, Federal funding for stem cell research had been banned. Many argued, however, that Federal funding for this research could lead to cures and treatments for terrible diseases. But the President recognized that providing Federal funds for research that destroys innocent human life would cross an unacceptable moral line.

To empower scientists and researchers without crossing that moral line, the President announced in August 2001 that Federal funds could be used for research on embryonic stem cell lines that already existed on the date of his announcement – making him the first President to provide Federal funding for embryonic stem cell research. However, he said that Federal funding for research using cell lines from embryos destroyed from that point forward would be banned.

In making this announcement, the President said: "I'm a strong supporter of science and technology .... I also believe human life is a sacred gift from our Creator ... and believe as your President I have an important obligation to foster and encourage respect for life in America and throughout the world.... Leading scientists tell me research on these 60 lines has great promise that could lead to breakthrough therapies and cures. This allows us to explore the promise and potential of stem cell research without crossing a fundamental moral line." More than $170 million in Federal funds have now been devoted to human embryonic stem cell research within these moral boundaries. In addition, more than $3.7 billion has gone to support innovative research on all forms of stem cells – including alternative techniques that could produce the functional equivalent of embryonic stem cells without the destruction of human life.

On more than one occasion, Congress tried to overturn the President's careful and balanced policy. In July 2006, Congress sent the President legislation that would have allowed the use of taxpayer money to fund the deliberate destruction of unborn life. The President vetoed the bill in the East Room of the White House, surrounded by families of "snowflake babies" – children who were adopted as frozen embryos and brought to term by loving parents.

A year later, Congress tried again to overturn the President's policy and once again the President sent the bill back with his veto. That same month, the President signed an Executive Order to expand support for non-destructive research methods. The order also converted the National Institutes of Health's embryonic stem cell registry into the "Human Pluripotent Stem Cell Registry," to reflect the value of the new cell lines produced without embryos.

In late 2007, two new studies were announced that demonstrated the potential of reprogramming adult cells, such as skin cells, to act like embryonic stem cells. With these advances, scientists now have the technology to create pluripotent stem cells, which have the added benefit of being genetically identical to the prospective patient.

In the President's final months in office, scientists succeeded in directly reprogramming one type of adult cell into another – without having to go through the intermediary step of reprogramming the cell back to a pluripotent or pseudo-embryonic state. With this advance, scientists have found a way to create the cells needed to develop new treatments and cures without using stem cells.

Scientists are putting these breakthroughs into action in an exciting new field called "regenerative medicine." To support these advances, the Administration announced the creation of a new Armed Forces Institute for Regenerative Medicine at the Department of Defense in April 2008. This new institute will partner with researchers at major academic and medical institutions to pioneer new methods of burn and wound repair; craniofacial reconstruction; limb reconstruction, regeneration, or transplantation; and other medical treatments that will benefit our soldiers and civilians alike.

Writing in the Washington Post, columnist Charles Krauthammer declared: "The verdict is clear: Rarely has a president – so vilified for a moral stance – been so thoroughly vindicated."

JUDGES

When President Bush ran for the White House, he argued that America needed judges who strictly interpret the Constitution, not ones who legislate from the bench. As he said in 2000: "I'll put competent judges on the bench. People who will strictly interpret the constitution and not use the bench for writing social policy.... I believe that judges ought not to take the place of the legislative branch of government."

During his eight years in office, President Bush kept that pledge. He appointed more than one-third of all active judges now sitting on the Federal bench – jurists of the highest caliber, with an abiding belief in the primacy of our Constitution.

His two most important judicial appointments were to the Supreme Court. In July 2005, Justice Sandra Day O'Connor announced her retirement, and the President nominated Judge John G. Roberts, Jr. of the D.C. Circuit Court of Appeals to the Supreme Court. Judge Roberts was an outstanding jurist who had clerked for then-Associate Justice William H. Rehnquist, served in the Office of Counsel to the President under President Reagan, and became one of the country's most experienced Supreme Court litigators.

Before Judge Roberts was confirmed, however, Chief Justice William Rehnquist passed away. President Bush decided to nominate Judge Roberts to be Chief Justice of the United States. At his confirmation hearing, Judge Roberts described his judicial philosophy this way: "Judges are like umpires. Umpires don't make the rules, they apply them. ... It is a limited role. Nobody ever went to a ball game to see the umpire." Judge Roberts was confirmed on September 29 by a vote of 78-22.

On October 3, President Bush announced he had chosen a lawyer he knew and trusted to fill Justice O'Connor's seat – Counsel to the President Harriet Miers. The Miers nomination met with opposition and some Senators demanded documents regarding the legal advice she provided the President, disclosures that would undermine a President's ability to receive candid counsel. After three weeks, Ms. Miers asked the President to withdraw her nomination.

The President then nominated Judge Samuel A. Alito, Jr. of the Third Circuit Court of Appeals to replace Justice O'Connor. On January 31, 2006, Judge Alito was confirmed as an Associate Justice by a vote of 58-42.

Many of the President's other nominees for the Federal bench were not afforded the fairness of an up-or-down vote. Miguel Estrada was one of the President's first nominees to the courts, and he had an inspiring personal history. He was an immigrant who came to the United States with little knowledge of English, worked his way to Harvard Law School, clerked at the Supreme Court, and served in the Justice Department under President Clinton. When Estrada was nominated for a seat on the D.C. Circuit Court of Appeals, he received a unanimous well-qualified rating from the American Bar Association. Yet for more than two years he awaited a vote in the Senate. He never got one. He endured years of delay, had his character unfairly attacked, and ultimately asked to be withdrawn from consideration.

Many other highly qualified judicial nominees endured similar uncertainty and withering attacks on their character simply because they accepted the call to public service. Some of these nominations were to vacancies designated "judicial emergencies," meaning that while these vacancies remained unfilled, legal disputes were left unresolved, the backlog of cases grew larger, and the rule of law was delayed for millions of Americans. The President said this failure to consider such qualified nominees was "a disgrace," "raw politics," and "bad for the country."

However, as the President prepared to leave office, 324 of his 377 nominees to Article III judicial positions had been confirmed by the Senate, and nearly one-third of his nominees were women and minorities. The confirmation process remains broken. Yet with his appointments of hundreds of outstanding jurists, President Bush has had a major impact on our Federal courts.

HEALTH CARE

When President Bush took office, some in our Nation's capital argued that government should make more health care decisions. The President placed his trust in a system of private medicine that has made America a world leader in health care – the Nation where people from around the globe come for the best doctors, newest treatments, latest technologies, and most advanced hospitals. His goal was to make this care more affordable and more accessible for Americans.

His Administration went about this in two ways. First, the President was determined to meet America's commitment to the poor and the elderly by strengthening Medicare and Medicaid and injecting market-based reforms into the programs. Second, he was determined to enact reforms to lower prices and give Americans access to less expensive and higher quality care.

Medicare Modernization and the Prescription Drug Benefit

On September 5, 2000, in Allentown, Pennsylvania, then-Governor Bush said, "[b]y history and by choice, our Nation makes a promise: We will honor our fathers and mothers by providing quality health insurance for every senior. Keeping the promise of Medicare and expanding it to include prescription drug coverage will be a priority of my Administration."

The President proposed a prescription drug benefit as part of a broader plan to address the long-term structural and fiscal problems in the Medicare program. In early 2003, he laid out the options that beneficiaries would be given under his Medicare plan:

- Stay in the existing program. Beneficiaries who chose this option would have access to discounted drugs, as well as coverage to protect against high out-of-pocket catastrophic costs – but would not have comprehensive drug coverage.

- Choose an Enhanced Medicare plan, which would give beneficiaries the same private health insurance choices available to Members of Congress and Federal employees. These plans would offer prescription drug benefits, full coverage of preventive benefits, and protection against high out-of-pocket costs.

- Choose Medicare Advantage, which would give beneficiaries options similar to private managed care plans, including a subsidized drug benefit.

Modifications were made to the Administration's proposal to provide all Medicare beneficiaries with the option to enroll in a private drug benefit plan. However, the Administration insisted that drug coverage only be provided by private plans without interference from the government in plan negotiations.

On December 8, 2003, President Bush signed the Medicare Prescription Drug Improvement and Modernization Act. Because of this law, more than 40 million Americans now have better access to prescription drugs. Nearly 10 million beneficiaries are now enrolled in private Medicare Advantage plans, which are available in every county in America. The legislation also provided low-income beneficiaries with additional help and ensured generic drugs would be brought to market sooner. The satisfaction rate among beneficiaries with the drug benefit is close to 90 percent.

The President's reforms injected market competition into the Medicare program. Largely as a result of this, the costs of the prescription drug plans have been far less than anticipated. The average prescription drug benefit premium for 2008 was nearly 40 percent lower than originally estimated and projected spending for the program's first ten years is approximately $240 billion less than originally anticipated. As the President stated, "[t]he lesson is when you trust people to make decisions in their life, when you have competition, it is likely you'll get lower price and better quality."

Medicaid

Like Medicare, Medicaid was in need of structural reform. This program was designed to provide certain groups of low-income and disabled Americans with medical insurance. While the program had a noble purpose, it was growing at an unsustainable rate and was not responsive to consumer needs.

In keeping with his philosophy of improving services and expanding choice, the President pushed for greater self-direction of Medicaid services. He called on Congress to pass the "Money Follows the Person" program to provide more home and community-based services, rather than institutional services. He signed the Deficit Reduction Act of 2005, which made this reform possible.

The Deficit Reduction Act also helped restrain Medicaid spending by reducing Federal overpayment for prescription drugs so that taxpayers would not have to pay inflated mark-ups. The law also gave governors more flexibility to design Medicaid benefits to meet their States' needs and tightened loopholes which had allowed some to game the system by transferring assets to their children so they could qualify for Medicaid benefits.

Community Health Centers

When President Bush came to office, one of the major strains on our health care system was the fact that many people often use emergency rooms for primary care. The President believed that one solution to this problem lay in expanding community health centers, which provide both primary and preventive health care services to patients who are uninsured or have inadequate health insurance.

In 2001, health centers across the country were serving 10 million patients. Within six years of taking office, the Bush Administration had funded more than 1,200 new or expanded health center sites around the country. These centers are now serving nearly 17 million patients, 91 percent of whom are low income.

Health Savings Accounts

For the majority of Americas who do not rely on Federal programs for their health insurance, the President embarked on a series of reforms to make private health insurance less expensive and give Americans greater choice. The President put individuals in charge of their own health care dollars by creating Health Savings Accounts (HSAs). With these accounts, instead of paying a large premium every month for services they may not use, individuals can pay a much smaller premium for major medical or catastrophic coverage – and then put the savings into a tax-free health account. Individuals can then use money from these accounts to pay for everyday medical expenses.

In 2003, HSAs were enacted into law as part of the Medicare Prescription Drug Improvement Act. In the first year HSAs were available, more than one-third of those who selected them had been uninsured, and one-third had incomes of less than $50,000. To further expand the use of HSAs, in 2006 President Bush signed the Tax Relief and Health Care Act, which raised contribution limits and made HSAs more flexible by allowing transfers from IRA accounts. These reforms encouraged even more people to sign up. By January 2008, 6.1 million people had HSA-qualified health plans. HSAs inject market forces into the health care system, which can help drive down costs.

Transparency and Information Technology Reforms

In order for individuals to be able to spend their HSA dollars wisely, they need to have better information about their health care options. So President Bush worked to infuse transparency into our health care system. In August 2006, the President signed an Executive Order directing Federal agencies that administer or sponsor Federal health insurance programs to increase transparency in pricing and quality.

The Bush Administration also worked to improve the use of information technology in the health care field to reduce medical errors, improve quality and efficiency, and save lives. In April 2004, the President announced the ambitious goal of assuring that most Americans have an electronic medical record within ten years. To help achieve this goal, the Federal Government took steps to encourage these efforts in the private sector, including adopting health information standards and supporting demonstration projects on health IT. The President also issued an Executive Order creating a new position within the Department of Health and Human Services charged with carrying out these efforts.

Mental Health Parity

On October 3, 2008, the President signed the Paul Wellstone and Peter Domenici Mental Health Parity and Addiction Equity Act. This law requires that mental health and substance-related disorder benefits are no more restrictive than those that apply to all medical and surgical benefits covered by group health plans that provide both. "Our country must make a commitment: Americans with mental illness deserve our understanding, and they deserve excellent care," the President said.

Genetic Information

With tremendous scientific advances in recent years – including the mapping of the human genome – previously unimagined genetic information became available to doctors, patients, and insurers. Believing this information should be used to prevent and treat disease, not deny patients needed coverage, the President called on Congress to protect the individual genetic information of every American. Working with the House and Senate, the President signed the Genetic Information Nondiscrimination Act of 2008, which prohibits health insurers and employers from discriminating on the basis of genetic information.

Other Health Reforms

In order to help small businesses and organizations cope with the spiraling cost of health care, the President called on Congress to pass legislation to allow for Association Health Plans (AHPs). AHPs allow small businesses and civic and community groups to join together to purchase health insurance and thus receive the same savings as large businesses. The President also called on Congress to pass medical liability reform to stop the spread of junk lawsuits that drive up insurance premiums and push good doctors out of practice.

These reforms could have reduced the ranks of the uninsured and made private insurance more affordable for Americans. Unfortunately, Congress failed to enact them. But by championing these reforms, President Bush laid the groundwork for future market-based reforms that preserve and strengthen our system of private medicine.

Reforming the Tax Code

The President's central proposal to make private health insurance more affordable was to reform the tax code. Under current law, workers who obtain their health insurance from their employers receive a tax benefit. However, most workers who buy insurance on their own get no tax benefit. The President believed this was unfair, so he proposed a policy to level the playing field. Under his proposal, every family with basic private health coverage of any cost would receive a standard deduction of $15,000. Families could exclude $15,000 from their income before they pay income or payroll taxes, no matter where they get their health insurance. The President also said that he was open to structuring the deduction as a tax credit instead. The President believed that new tax incentives for health insurance would lead more Americans to buy coverage through the private health insurance market. By reforming the tax code, more than 100 million people who are now covered by employer-provided insurance would have seen reduced tax bills. And as many as 20 million others who have no health insurance would have been able to purchase basic coverage.

SCHIP

One important commitment of the Federal Government is to help America's poorest children get access to health care. Most of these children are covered by Medicaid. For poor children who do not qualify for Medicaid, there is a program called the State Children's Health Insurance Program (SCHIP).

The President strongly supported SCHIP during his time in office, adding more than 2.5 million children to the program since 2001. And the President's 2008 budget proposed increasing SCHIP funding by $5 billion over five years – a 20 percent increase.

Unfortunately, the program was in need of reform. More than 500,000 poor children who were eligible for SCHIP coverage were not enrolled. At the same time, many States were spending SCHIP funds on adults. In 2007, Minnesota, Illinois, New Jersey, Michigan, Wisconsin, and New Mexico spent more SCHIP money on adults than children.

Congressional Democrats developed a plan to expand SCHIP in ways the program was never intended. Their legislation would have raised spending by $35 to $50 billion, and paid for it by raising taxes on working Americans. Their proposal would have turned a program meant to help poor children into one covering children in some households with incomes of up to $83,000 a year. And their proposal would have moved millions of children who already had private health insurance into a government-run insurance program.

The President said that "Congress' SCHIP plan is an incremental step toward ... government-run health care for every American," but he offered to work with Congress to increase funding for SCHIP beyond the 20 percent in his budget request, as long as the bill did not raise taxes, and as long as the increased funds went to help poor children. In his 2009 Budget, the President proposed adding $19 billion to SCHIP over 5 years –a nearly 70 percent increase over the baseline. In October 2007, Congress sent the President a deeply flawed bill, and the President vetoed it.

After his veto, the President again expressed his willingness to work with Congress to find common ground, but in early December 2007, they sent the President an essentially identical bill. So he vetoed it again, and once again his veto was sustained. Later in the month, the President signed a bill to extend the existing SCHIP program until April 2009 and prevent an interruption of coverage for those already enrolled in the program. The President stuck to his principles, and his record on children's health is outstanding. According to one study, the number of uninsured children under 18 declined by 800,000 between 2001 and 2007.

By focusing on practical, market-based solutions, the Bush Administration delivered genuine health care reform. Government programs such as Medicare are more responsive and on a better footing. Medicare beneficiaries have prescription drug benefits. Americans have more affordable choices in private insurance thanks to initiatives such as HSAs. And the health care system is being modernized through the adoption of information technologies and increased transparency in pricing and quality.

Avian Flu and Pandemic Influenza

The danger of avian and pandemic influenza is a significant threat. In 2005, the President announced a comprehensive national strategy to prepare for an influenza pandemic.

That year, the President launched the International Partnership on Avian and Pandemic Influenza to coordinate efforts among donor and affected nations, increase transparency in disease reporting, and build local capacity to respond to an influenza pandemic. More than 120 countries and 26 international organizations have joined the effort, and the United States has contributed nearly $1 billion to help these foreign partners take vital actions to detect and contain outbreaks. And to strengthen domestic surveillance, the Administration launched the National Bio-surveillance Initiative – an effort to rapidly detect, quantify, and respond to outbreaks of disease, and deliver information quickly to State, local, national, and international public health officials.

The President took action to stockpile vaccines and antiviral drugs and accelerate development of new vaccine technologies needed to combat a pandemic. If a pandemic were to occur, there may not be a vaccine available for the first several months capable of fully immunizing our citizens. To help protect our citizens during these early months, Federal researchers developed a vaccine based on the current strain of the avian flu virus, and at the Administration's urging Congress approved funds to purchase enough doses to vaccinate 20 million people.

The Administration also secured Congressional approval to stockpile additional antiviral medications that can reduce the severity of the illness. The United States now has enough of these antiviral drugs on hand to help treat first responders and those on the front lines, as well as populations most at risk in the first stages of a pandemic.

The Administration also worked to put in place a surge capacity to allow us to bring a new vaccine online quickly and manufacture enough to immunize every American. To ensure local communities are ready in the event of a pandemic, the President worked with Congress to obtain $600 million for pandemic preparedness, including $150 million to help States complete and exercise their pandemic plans. At the President's direction, the Federal Government stockpiled critical supplies such as syringes, hospital beds, respirators, masks, and protective equipment in locations across America.

The steps the President took will help safeguard the American people in the event of a devastating global pandemic, and will strengthen our ability to produce vaccines for pandemic influenza and a range of other illnesses. And they will help our Nation prepare for other dangers such as a terrorist attack using chemical or biological weapons.

ENERGY SECURITY
&
CLIMATE CHANGE

Energy Security

One of the President's first priorities was to take on the challenge of energy security. Immediately after taking office, he asked Vice President Cheney to lead the effort to develop a national energy strategy, and in May 2001, the Vice President submitted a report with more than 100 policy recommendations. For four years, Congress discussed and debated the Administration's proposals with no result. In 2005, having won a second term, the President began a new push for energy legislation. Congress eventually passed two major laws that contained many elements of the President's strategy. On August 8, 2005, the President signed the Energy Policy Act – the first major energy legislation in more than a decade. And on December 19, 2007, the President signed the Energy Independence and Security Act.

These two laws, together with other executive actions, helped the Administration address the energy challenges facing our country. The President explained one of the core problems in his 2006 State of the Union address. "America," the President declared, "is addicted to oil." This dependence harms America economically through high and volatile prices at the gas pump; creates pollution and contributes to greenhouse gas emissions; and threatens America's national security by making us vulnerable to hostile regimes in unstable regions of the world.

The President argued that the best way to break this addiction and confront climate change is through advances in clean and renewable energy technologies. His Administration worked to promote these advances by transforming the ways Americans fuel their cars and trucks and transforming the ways Americans power their homes and offices.

To transform the way Americans fuel their cars and trucks, the Administration worked to reduce gasoline consumption and promote alternative fuels. The 2005 Energy Policy Act established a national alternative fuels standard to encourage greater use of renewable fuels like ethanol and biodiesel. To make further progress, the President proposed an aggressive plan to reduce projected gasoline consumption by 20 percent over 10 years – his "Twenty-in-Ten" plan. The 2007 Energy Independence and Security Act didn't go as far as the President's plan, but it specified a national, mandatory fuel economy standard of 35 miles per gallon by 2020 – which will save billions of gallons of fuel. This legislation also required the use of at least 36 billion gallons of renewable fuel in the year 2022 – a nearly five-fold increase over the previous mandate.

The Administration provided strong support for the development and production of alternative fuels. One promising alternative fuel is biodiesel, which can be produced from soybeans, vegetable oils, and waste products like recycled cooking grease. In 2007, America produced approximately 450 million gallons of biodiesel, an increase of 80 percent from 2006 levels. Today, there are more than 650 biodiesel fueling stations, and hundreds of fleet operators use biodiesel to fuel their trucks.

Under the President's leadership, ethanol production quadrupled from 1.6 billion gallons in 2000 to nearly 6.5 billion gallons in 2007. In 2005, the United States became the world's leading ethanol producer, and today America accounts for nearly half of worldwide ethanol production.

Most of this ethanol comes from corn. To expand and diversify the supply of ethanol, the Administration also invested in research and development into cellulosic ethanol, which can be made from wood chips, switch grass, and other agricultural products and leads to significantly lower greenhouse gas emissions. The Administration dedicated approximately $1 billion to develop technologies that can make cellulosic ethanol cost-competitive. Since 2001, the projected cost of cellulosic ethanol has dropped more than 60 percent.

The President also worked to expand the number of vehicles that use alternative sources of energy. The Administration promoted hybrid vehicles that run on both gasoline and electricity by providing tax incentives for people to buy these vehicles and $25 billion in loans to re-tool factories to make them. When the President took office in 2001, there were few hybrids on the roads. Today, there are more than a million. The Administration also invested in research into new battery technologies for plug-in hybrid cars. In 2003, the Administration launched the Hydrogen Fuel Initiative to develop technologies for hydrogen-powered fuel cell vehicles that use no gasoline at all, and emit clean, pure water. Over the past five years, the U.S. Government has invested approximately $1.2 billion in research and development to help bring these technologies to market.

As the Administration pursued these long-term initiatives, the President recognized that, in the short-term, the United States would have to rely on oil for most of its fuel supply. So in 2008, he urged Congress to expand domestic production of oil by removing barriers that made many domestic oil deposits off-limits for exploration and production. The President removed the executive restrictions on offshore exploration on the Outer Continental Shelf (OCS). And he called on Congress to lift legislative restrictions on this exploration. He also renewed calls for Congress to expand American oil production by tapping into the extraordinary potential of oil shale – a type of rock that can produce oil when exposed to heat or other processes; to permit environmentally sensitive exploration in the Arctic National Wildlife Refuge (ANWR) in northern Alaska; and to expand and enhance America's domestic refining capacity by expediting the refinery permitting process. Though Congress did not permit exploration in ANWR or improve the refinery permitting process, it removed its ban on responsible exploration on the OCS and expanded access to oil shale – clearing the way for increased domestic oil production.

The President also worked to renew investment in an important alternative energy source – nuclear power. When the President entered office, this country had not started construction on a new nuclear power plant in more than 20 years due to obstacles such as excessive regulation and potential lawsuits. To help address these concerns, the Administration requested, and Congress approved, a Federal risk insurance program to help protect the owners of plants against lawsuits, bureaucratic obstacles, and other delays beyond their control. The Administration also launched the Nuclear Power 2010 program, a partnership between industry and the U.S. Government to encourage the construction of new plants. These programs, along with other significant Administration efforts, helped encourage industry to submit 17 applications to build and operate 26 new nuclear reactors in the United States. Those advanced nuclear power plants are eligible to apply for $18.5 billion in loan guarantees provided by the Energy Policy Act of 2005. If exercised, these Federal Government guarantees will enable nuclear plant owners to reduce their interest costs, making nuclear power cheaper for American consumers. Because of the President's leadership, America is on the cusp of a renaissance in this key, emissions-free power source.

In 2007 and 2008, the Administration invested more than $730 million in research and development of nuclear energy technologies. And to make these technologies more widely available, the Administration created the Global Nuclear Energy Partnership, which is working with 21 countries to help enable the expansion of civilian nuclear energy while decreasing the risk of nuclear weapons proliferation and addressing the challenge of nuclear waste disposal.

The Administration also expanded other alternative sources of electricity. Since the President took office in 2001, America has increased wind energy production by more than 400 percent. In 2007, more than 30 percent of new electrical generating capacity in America came from wind – up from just three percent in 2001. And in 2007, America installed more wind power capacity than any other country in the world.

The President also created the Solar America Initiative in 2006 – a program to accelerate the development of solar technology, with the goal of making solar power cost competitive with other forms of renewable electricity by 2015. The Administration has invested more than $1 billion in solar research and development. New solar projects are among those being supported by $10 billion in loan guarantees for advanced renewable technologies and substantial production incentives. America's solar energy capacity more than doubled during the President's term – and in 2007, U.S. solar installations grew by more than 30 percent.

The President worked to expand the use of our most abundant energy resource, coal, and to ensure that coal will be an environmentally-friendly source of energy. The Bush Administration invested more than $2.5 billion into clean coal research and development. In 2008, the Administration also made available more than $8 billion in loan guarantees that will support new projects to produce power from coal with low greenhouse gas emissions. And in his 2009 budget, the President requested nearly $650 million for advanced coal research – the largest such request in more than 25 years. This funding would support the development of technology to capture the carbon dioxide emissions that come from coal. These advances could dramatically reduce coal's impact on the environment, which may eventually allow us to prevent 90 percent of coal's carbon emissions from being released into the environment.

This broad array of policies and actions helped America meet its immediate energy needs, while investing in clean energy technologies that will increase America's energy security in the decades to come.

Climate Change

The President's climate strategy was based on a clear principle: the best way to confront climate change is by ushering in a new era of clean energy technology.

When President Bush took office, the United States was under pressure from many in the international community to ratify a flawed treaty called the Kyoto Protocol. The Kyoto Protocol would have required the U.S. and other developed nations to drastically reduce greenhouse gas emissions, while allowing major developing economies, like China and India, to increase their emissions. According to some estimates, the treaty would have cost the United States up to $400 billion, and resulted in the loss of up to 4.9 million jobs. And because the treaty did not include the largest emitters, it would not have reduced overall greenhouse gas emissions.

Upon taking office, President Bush adopted a balanced approach to climate change. Domestically, his Administration pursued a comprehensive blend of market incentives and regulations to reduce greenhouse gas emissions and encourage the development of clean and efficient energy technologies. And internationally, the Administration worked to involve all major economies in the effort to address global climate change – while increasing the access of developing nations to the advanced clean energy technologies needed to control greenhouse gas emissions.

The President put America on a path to slow, stop, and eventually reverse the growth of its greenhouse gas emissions. In 2002, he set a goal of reducing America's greenhouse gas emissions intensity by 18 percent through 2012. To help achieve this goal, his Administration committed $22 billion between 2001 and 2008 to climate change technology research and deployment – more than any other country in the world. And by 2007, America's greenhouse gas intensity had declined by nearly 10 percent from 2002 levels, well on track to reach the President's goal.

To build on this progress, in 2008 the President announced a new national goal: to stop the growth of U.S. greenhouse gas emissions by 2025, and begin to reverse them thereafter. To help reach this goal, the Administration promoted an economy-wide strategy that combines new market-based regulations, new government incentives, and new funding for technology research. The Administration invested in research to develop and commercially deploy clean and efficient energy technologies; worked with Congress to enact new fuel economy and alternative fuel standards; mandated new objectives for the coming decade to increase the efficiency of lighting and appliances; worked to help States achieve their goals for increasing renewable power and building code efficiency by sharing new technologies and providing tax incentives; dedicated billions of dollars in Farm Bill conservation programs to help biologically sequester greenhouse gas emissions; and worked with Congress to make available more than $40 billion in loan guarantees to support investments that will avoid, reduce, or sequester greenhouse gas emissions or air pollutants.

These landmark actions will prevent billions of metric tons of greenhouse gas emissions from entering the atmosphere.

As the President took these steps at home, he also rallied other nations to address the challenge of global climate change. As the President put it, "even if we reduced our own emissions to zero tomorrow, we would not make a meaningful dent in solving the problem without concerted action by all major economies." In September 2007, the Administration launched – and the G-8 endorsed – the Major Economies Meeting process, which brings together the world's biggest energy consumers and greenhouse gas emitters in a dialogue that encourages meaningful participation of every major economy, and contributes to negotiations on a global climate agreement under the UN Framework Convention on Climate Change once the Kyoto Protocol expires in 2012.

That same month, the Administration achieved one the most significant international breakthroughs in the effort to stem emissions of greenhouse gases, concluding a new international agreement under the Montreal Protocol that will accelerate cuts in hydrochlorofluorocarbon (HCFC) refrigerant emissions. HCFCs are an extremely potent greenhouse gas, and this agreement is projected to prevent more HCFCs from going into the atmosphere than the Kyoto Protocol, possibly by a factor of three or four.

The Administration also worked to promote and support deployment of clean energy and other climate change technologies in developing countries. In July 2005, the Administration launched the Asia Pacific Partnership on Clean Development and Climate (APP). This partnership includes seven nations – the United States, Australia, Canada, China, India, Japan, and South Korea – that together represent nearly half of the world's economy, population, and energy use. Through the APP, these countries are working together on practical ways to accelerate the development and deployment of clean energy technologies that will dramatically reduce greenhouse gas emissions. And in July 2008, the United States worked with its G-8 partners to establish a new International Clean Technology Fund to support the use of clean energy technology across the world.

With these and other international efforts, the Bush Administration has successfully transformed the climate change debate to include not only industrialized countries, but also major emerging economies, in a common effort to lower greenhouse gas emissions.

The Bush Administration invested more than $44 billion to advance climate related science, technology, observation, and incentives. The President also signed legislation giving the Department of Energy the authority to provide more than $67 billion in loans and guarantees to help support innovative energy projects to reduce greenhouse gas or air pollutant emissions and to retool auto plants to produce more efficient vehicles. While U.S. greenhouse gas emissions increased by 14.2 percent in absolute terms through the 1990s, net greenhouse gas emissions declined by three percent between 2000 and 2006.

ENVIRONMENT
&
CONSERVATION

Urban Environment

Under the Bush Administration, air pollution was cut 12 percent from 2001 to 2007. And to build on this progress, the Administration finalized new rules that will cut hazardous emissions from 80 industrial sources, diesel engine emissions by more than 90 percent, and power plant emissions by nearly 70 percent.

In 2002, the President signed legislation to clean up abandoned and polluted industrial sites known as brownfields. Since then, the Administration has provided more than $1 billion for brownfield revitalization and leveraged an additional $11.4 billion from private and other sources for this effort. As a result, more than 11,000 brownfields sites have been given a clean bill of health for new investment. These efforts opened usable land for small businesses and residents in communities across the country.

Ocean Conservation

The President made ocean conservation an important priority, and launched an Ocean Action Plan in 2004 to make America's oceans, coasts, and Great Lakes cleaner, healthier, and more productive. Under the Ocean Action Plan, the Bush Administration worked to stop overfishing. In 2007, the President issued an Executive Order protecting two of our Nation's most popular game fish – striped bass and red drum. The President also signed important legislation reauthorizing the Magnuson Stevens Act – which sets a firm deadline to end overfishing in America by 2011.

The Administration also took action to protect and restore vital marine habitats. In 2004, the Administration set a goal of restoring, improving, and protecting three million acres of interior and coastal wetlands in five years – and met that goal one year ahead of schedule.

During the past eight years, the Bush Administration also put two-thirds of Federal waters – approximately 2.3 million square nautical miles – off-limits to harmful bottom-trawling and dredging. The Administration made a special effort to protect coral reefs. Some of the most spectacular reefs are found within the Papahānaumokuākea Marine National Monument, which the President created in June 2006. This monument in the Northwestern Hawaiian Islands is the world's largest fully protected marine conservation area, and protects more than 7,000 marine species – a quarter of which are found nowhere else on earth. It is also on track to become a UNESCO World Heritage site – the first U.S. site in 15 years.

The President increased international cooperation to protect the ocean environment. Through the Coral Triangle Initiative, the Administration worked with nations like Indonesia, Malaysia, the Philippines, and Australia to identify and eliminate the threats to tropical reefs. And at the United Nations, the Administration succeeded in passing a resolution to help protect fish stocks and marine habitats from destructive fishing practices.

The President expanded ocean research. In January 2007, the Administration launched a Ten Year Ocean Research Priorities Plan. Research supported by the plan is helping to reduce shipping's impact on the environment; improve understanding of important ocean conditions like red tides and the ocean's role in climate change; and improve our ability to protect Americans from natural disasters like hurricanes and tsunamis.

The President expanded education programs to teach citizens more about our oceans. Mrs. Bush undertook an effort to educate young people about the importance of our oceans and the harmful effects of marine debris. And the Administration launched the Coastal Ecosystem Learning Center Network, which is helping the public learn hands-on about sea life at more than 20 of America's top aquariums, as well as the new Sant Ocean Hall at the Smithsonian's National Museum of Natural History, which President Bush dedicated in 2008.

In his final months in office, the President took additional steps to improve the environment. He launched an initiative to protect, restore, and improve an additional four million acres of wetlands. He expanded the Monterey Bay National Marine Sanctuary to include the Davidson Seamount. This 585-square-nautical-mile addition will safeguard one of the largest known seamounts in U.S. waters, and protect an extraordinary array of ocean creatures.

He also designated three beautiful and biologically-diverse areas of the Pacific Ocean as new marine national monuments:

1. The Marianas Trench Marine National Monument, a unique geological region more than five times longer than the Grand Canyon, which includes the majestic coral reefs off the coast of the upper three islands in the Commonwealth of the Northern Mariana Islands.

2. The Pacific Remote Islands Marine National Monument, which spans seven areas to the far south and west of Hawaii and includes some of the most pristine and spectacular coral reefs in the world.

3. The Rose Atoll Marine National Monument, a diamond-shaped island to the east of American Samoa that includes rare species of nesting petrels, shearwaters, and terns, and whose waters are also home to many rare species, including giant clams and reef sharks.

Taken together, these three new national monuments cover nearly 200,000 square miles, and they will now receive our Nation's highest level of environmental recognition and conservation.

Wildlife Conservation

The President also took decisive action to promote wildlife habitats through a policy of cooperative conservation. Under this approach, the Federal Government worked in a spirit of respect and cooperation with those seeking to protect our land, sea, and sky. Cooperative conservation respects the unique knowledge of local authorities, and welcomes the help of private groups and volunteers.

Using this cooperative conservation approach, the Bush Administration worked with America's hunters and sportsmen to set clear goals, enhance habitats, conserve wildlife populations, and increase opportunities for hunting.

The President worked to protect wildlife in America's forests. During the past eight years, the U.S. Forest Service partnered with hunting organizations to improve the food supply for animals in America's national forests. This has enhanced habitats for game species such as elk, deer, wild turkeys, and waterfowl. The Forest Service has also joined with State wildlife agencies, conservation groups, and individual citizens to return thousands of wild turkeys to Federal lands. And in 2002, the President launched the Healthy Forest Initiative to help prevent catastrophic wildfires. Since the Initiative began, the Forest Service thinned and removed underbrush across more than 27 million acres – protecting animal habitats and hunting grounds.

The Administration increased funding to operate our national parks by more than 40 percent since 2001 – including funds for the restoration of a variety of wildlife habitats. And in February 2007, the President launched the National Parks Centennial Initiative so that we can improve our national parks in time for their 100th anniversary in 2016. The President also worked to protect and improve habitat for migratory birds in our national parks.

The President encouraged landowners to increase wildlife populations on private property. The Administration expanded Federal tax incentives to encourage landowners to donate their property for the purpose of conservation. And through the Conservation Reserve Program, the Administration helped ranchers and farmers restore grassland habitats on their land. Since 2001, the Administration has enrolled approximately 12.6 million acres in the program – and created important nesting habitats for game birds like pheasant and quail.

The President also worked to ensure that America's sportsmen, hunters, and conservationists can make responsible use of Federal lands. Since 2001, the Bush Administration has opened up 30 National Wildlife Refuges to hunting and worked with 40 sportsmen's groups to improve access to hunting and fishing on Federal property.

DISASTER RESPONSE

During the past eight years, the Bush Administration responded to more than 900 natural disasters across the United States – including wildfires, floods, tornadoes, severe winter storms, and hurricanes. In almost every case, the Federal Government's response was effective, providing our citizens with the shelter and support they needed to get through the crisis. One storm was so massive, however, that it overwhelmed our government's disaster relief system and exposed weaknesses in our government's ability to respond to catastrophic events.

Hurricane Katrina

On August 29, 2005, Hurricane Katrina made landfall along the Gulf Coast. The storm affected nearly 93,000 square miles, an area roughly the size of Great Britain. It left 80 percent of New Orleans, Louisiana, underwater, and forced 800,000 people across the Gulf Coast to leave their homes.

The storm and subsequent flooding laid bare flaws in Federal, State, and local preparedness. Speaking to the Nation from Jackson Square on September 15, the President said: "Four years after the frightening experience of September 11, Americans have every right to expect a more effective response in a time of emergency. When the Federal Government fails to meet such an obligation, I, as President, am responsible for the problem, and for the solution." He promised a comprehensive review of the response of Hurricane Katrina so the Federal Government could improve its emergency response capabilities and ensure our Nation is "better prepared for any challenge of nature or act of evil men that could threaten our people." And he made the people of the Gulf Coast this pledge: "Throughout the area hit by the hurricane, we will do what it takes; we will stay as long as it takes to help citizens rebuild their communities and their lives."

The Bush Administration followed through on this pledge, providing more than $126 billion for disaster response and recovery on the Gulf Coast. The Army Corps of Engineers repaired 220 miles of the levees – and began upgrading the floodwalls to make them stronger

115

than before Katrina. The Department of Health and Human Services provided more than $2.6 billion to care for the poor and uninsured, provide mental-health services, and support primary-care clinics and hospitals. The Department of Education helped more than 80 public schools in the city reopen – with approximately half of those becoming charter schools.

The Administration retooled and restructured the Federal Emergency Management Agency (FEMA) – improving FEMA's logistics management; strengthening its operations planning; augmenting its disaster assistance programs; and providing the agency with additional personnel and resources. The Department of Homeland Security created a National Operations Center to serve as the coordination center for ensuring an integrated, interagency response to a disaster. The Department of Health and Human Services was given a new mission to lead the Federal Government's medical response to a crisis. The Department of Housing and Urban Development worked with FEMA to establish the Disaster Housing Assistance Program. The Department of Justice improved its capabilities to coordinate Federal law enforcement support during a disaster. And the Department of Defense improved its disaster response capabilities, preparing pre-drafted mission orders that can be executed almost immediately in case of a major event, and improving its integration with FEMA and other Federal agencies.

Before the President left office, the Federal Government's improved disaster response capabilities were put to the test, including when Hurricanes Gustav and Ike hit the Gulf Coast in 2008. The rebuilt levees in New Orleans held. And the Federal Government was able to rapidly evacuate nearly two million people. Because of the Bush Administration's efforts, the Federal Government is better prepared to deal with any disaster that might befall our Nation – be it an act of man or an act of nature. And because of the President's commitment, the City of New Orleans and communities along the Gulf Coast are recovering and rebuilding.

IMMIGRATION AND
SOCIAL SECURITY

Immigration and Social Security were two pressing challenges that the President addressed. While the President was unable to secure passage of reform legislation in these areas, he laid the groundwork for future presidents and congresses to solve these challenges.

Immigration

Immigration reform was one of the President's principal domestic policy goals. His first foreign visit was to Mexico, where he discussed immigration issues with President Vicente Fox. But the 9/11 attacks delayed discussion of comprehensive immigration reform as the Administration focused on border security and interior enforcement.

In January 2004, the President took up the issue of immigration once again. In a speech at the White House, the President laid out a proposal for comprehensive reform. The centerpiece of the plan was a new temporary worker program that would be open to both new foreign workers and undocumented individuals already in the United States. The President declared his opposition to amnesty, which he defined as an automatic path to citizenship. A few weeks later, he made immigration reform a central focus of his State of the Union address. However, by spring it became clear that there would be no action in Congress before the November presidential election.

The House passed an immigration reform bill in December 2005 that focused on border security, more effective civil enforcement of existing immigration laws, and increased criminal sanctions for immigration-related crimes. In the spring of 2006, as the Senate debated a broader reform bill that included a temporary worker program, the President delivered a prime time address to the Nation on immigration from the Oval Office. The President announced that he was deploying 6,000 members of the National Guard to the southern border and reemphasized his five key objectives for immigration reform: improved border security; better interior enforcement; a new temporary worker program; new measures to encourage assimilation; and a way forward to resolve the status of those here illegally. The temporary worker program would create a legal path for foreign workers to enter the United States in an orderly way, for a limited period of time. This program would match willing foreign works with willing American employers for jobs Americans were not doing. The President also proposed that illegal immigrants who have roots in the United States and want to stay should pay a meaningful penalty for breaking the law, pay their taxes, learn English, and maintain a steady job. People who met these conditions would be able to apply for citizenship, but approval would not be automatic, and they would have to wait in line behind those who played by the rules and followed the law.

Ten days later, the Senate passed a comprehensive immigration reform bill by a vote of 62-36. But this bill was never passed by the full Congress. Congress focused its attention on enforcement, and in October, the President signed the Secure Fence Act of 2006, which authorized the construction of hundreds of miles of additional fencing along the Southern border, as well as vehicle barriers, checkpoints, and advanced technology to stop illegal crossings.

The President continued to make the case that our country could never fully secure our border until it created a lawful way for foreign workers to come to the United States and support our economy. In 2007, he made another push for immigration reform and after months of negotiation, an agreement was finally reached with a bipartisan group of senators. The bill included security and enforcement benchmarks that would have to be met before other elements of the program were implemented. Once those goals were met, the plan would have created a temporary worker program to allow workers to come to the United States for a short period of time and fill jobs Americans were not doing. For immigrants wishing to come to the United States permanently, it would have established a new merit-based system that would have taken into account job skills, education, English proficiency, and family ties. The plan would have brought undocumented workers already in the country out of the shadows without amnesty and without animosity. It would have required workers to pay a meaningful penalty, learn English, pay their taxes, and pass a background check before they could be considered for legalized status. If they achieved this legalized status and wanted to apply for a green card, they would then have to return home to file an application and get in line behind those who followed the law.

This bipartisan compromise, however, failed in the Congress. After Congress failed to act, the President announced 26 immigration reforms the Administration would undertake on its own. Twenty-four of these were carried out, and two were partially completed. While the President will leave office without signing a comprehensive immigration bill into law, he will leave behind many accomplishments – including doubling the size of the Border Patrol, building hundreds of miles of border fence, vastly improving enforcement of immigration law, streamlining guest-worker programs, and improving measures for assimilating new immigrants. The President's leadership on this issue, and the legislative compromise he forged in 2007, will serve as a model for future reform efforts.

Social Security

The President also led on the issue of reforming Social Security. When Social Security was created, there were approximately 40 workers paying Social Security taxes for every one retiree receiving benefits. By 2001, it was down to only about three workers and over the decades to come, that number will fall to just two workers per beneficiary. And because people now live longer, they also draw benefits longer, which means benefits will rise dramatically over the next few decades. As a result, Social Security will soon be paying out more than it takes in. If steps were not taken now, the President said, the shortfalls would grow dramatically, and the only solutions would be drastically higher taxes, massive new borrowing, or sudden and severe cuts in benefits.

The President made Social Security reform a centerpiece of both of his presidential campaigns. In 2000, he laid out his principles for reform, including the establishment of voluntary personal accounts; the preservation of Social Security's disability and survivors' components; and a pledge not to raise payroll taxes, change benefits for those near retirement, or invest the Social Security Trust Fund in the stock market. Like many other initiatives, Social Security reform was temporarily derailed by the 9/11 attacks. But in 2004, the President once again campaigned on a promise to reform Social Security. And in his first press conference after being elected to a second term, the President promised that "reforming Social Security will be a priority of my Administration."

In fixing Social Security, the President faced a challenge. He had previously set a goal of cutting the deficit in half by 2009. This complicated his Social Security efforts, because in the near-term, creating personal accounts would worsen the budget balance. To reduce the near-term cost, the President decided to phase-in personal accounts over three years. This gradual approach helped keep the near-term budget impact of the proposal down, but made it less attractive to the American people. On the matter of solvency, the President laid out a principle that payroll taxes must not be raised, and offered a menu of options that he would consider. He announced his Social Security plan in his 2005 State of the Union address, and then embarked on a "Sixty Stops in Sixty Days" tour to discuss it across the country.

In April 2005, the President endorsed an approach to bringing the system into solvency put forward by a former Democratic member of the Social Security Commission, Robert Pozen. The Pozen plan called for "progressive indexation" of Social Security. Under the plan, benefits for the poorest 30 percent of workers would continue to be tied to wages. For the highest earning Americans, benefits would be linked to inflation, which grows at a slower rate than wages. And for all those in between, benefits would grow at a rate higher than inflation. This approach would have fixed at least two-thirds of the long-term Social Security problem without tax increases of any kind, while protecting the lowest-income workers. Unfortunately, Congress failed to act.

According to the most recent Social Security Trustees report, Social Security will experience its first permanent cash deficits in 2017. President Bush warned that the system is headed toward bankruptcy and did everything in his power to address the problem during his time in office.

THE FIRST LADY'S LEADERSHIP

Education

As a former librarian and teacher, Mrs. Bush adopted literacy and education as signature issues during her tenure in the East Wing. Only weeks after arriving in Washington, she launched a new education initiative – "Ready to Read, Ready to Learn." This effort sought to prepare children for success in school and ensure that all students have well-trained, qualified teachers.

In July 2001, Mrs. Bush began her work toward these goals by hosting the White House Summit on Early Childhood Cognitive Development. In addition, she initiated the publication of the Healthy Start, Grow Smart magazine series, which outlines activities to stimulate infant brain development and build the skills that children need to begin school. In March 2002, Mrs. Bush organized the White House Conference on Preparing Tomorrow's Teachers, which followed the passage of the No Child Left Behind Act. Mrs. Bush was a key advocate for this new law, and she helped shape No Child Left Behind's Reading First program, which is the largest early reading initiative in our Nation's history.

Helping America's Youth

At the beginning of his second term, President Bush announced the Helping America's Youth initiative and asked Mrs. Bush to lead it. Over the next three years, Mrs. Bush traveled the Nation to highlight the work of effective community youth programs, including mentoring, sports, job training, and gang prevention programs. These visits led to the White House Conference on Helping America's Youth in October 2005, and then to six regional conferences in Indianapolis, Denver, Nashville, St. Paul, Dallas, and Portland

In addition, Federal agencies worked together to develop the Community Guide to Helping America's Youth, a valuable online tool to help communities evaluate their assets, identify local and Federal resources, and get information about proven programs to support at-risk youth. In

February 2008, the President signed an Executive Order that established the Interagency Working Group on Youth Programs, continuing this successful collaboration of Federal youth-serving agencies.

Afghanistan

Two months after the 9/11 attacks, Mrs. Bush delivered the President's weekly radio address. She used the air time to speak out about the oppression of women and children under the Taliban. Over the next seven years, Mrs. Bush met frequently with Afghan women, elected officials, teachers, students, and entrepreneurs. She became the Honorary Chair of the U.S.-Afghan Women's Council, which President Bush and Afghan President Hamid Karzai established in 2002.

In March 2005, Mrs. Bush surprised the world by joining the Council for an unannounced visit to Kabul. She toured the National Women's Dormitory and the Women's Teacher Training Institute – two Council initiatives at Kabul University. Mrs. Bush also announced funding from the United States government to support the American University of Afghanistan and the International School of Kabul.

Mrs. Bush returned to Kabul with the President a year later. And in June 2008, she went on her third trip to the Afghan capital, where she met with students at the schools whose construction she had helped support three years earlier. In Bamiyan Province, she joined Afghanistan's first female governor to discuss the progress of women's rights with female police officers and meet future students of a school under construction through the U.S.-Afghan Women's Council. Mrs. Bush also helped establish a partnership between the U.S.-Afghan Women's Council and Georgetown University, which has given the Council a permanent home within the university community.

Global Literacy

Worldwide, more than 770 million adults live without literacy skills. In 2003, Mrs. Bush traveled to Paris to reopen the United States' mission to UNESCO. She also began addressing the global literacy crisis as Honorary Ambassador for the United Nations Literacy Decade (UNLD). In this role, she convened education ministers, literacy experts, and leaders from around the world for annual meetings, beginning with the White House Conference on Global Literacy in 2006. This effort inspired six subsequent UNESCO regional conferences over a two-year period in Qatar, Mali, India, China, Azerbaijan, and Mexico. The 2008 White House Symposium on Advancing Global Literacy brought together representatives from all six host nations to share outcomes from the UNESCO regional conferences and chart the way forward in expanding literacy to all. Mrs. Bush accepted an invitation to continue serving as Honorary Ambassador to the UNLD through 2012.

Mrs. Bush was also an outspoken ambassador for the President's international education programs. She placed special emphasis on programs supported by the Africa Education Initiative (AEI) during her five trips to Africa. Mrs. Bush supported these efforts by visiting teacher training programs, distributing textbooks at local schools, and announcing new scholarships through AEI's Ambassadors' Girls Scholarship Program.

Health and Women's Wellness

Mrs. Bush's worked to raise awareness about breast cancer and heart disease in women and to stop the global spread of diseases like HIV/AIDS and malaria. In 2006, Mrs. Bush announced a groundbreaking partnership between the U.S. Department of State, the Susan G. Komen Foundation, the M.D. Anderson Cancer Center, the Johns Hopkins University, and both the United Arab Emirates (UAE) and the Kingdom of Saudi Arabia. Known as the U.S.-Middle East Partnership for Breast Cancer Awareness and Research, the Partnership has since expanded to include Jordan and the Palestinian Territories. Mrs. Bush traveled to the UAE, Saudi Arabia, and Jordan to promote the Partnership and participated in community discussions about breast cancer and visited treatment and screening sites. One of Mrs. Bush's stops took her to the Abdullatif Cancer Screening Center in Riyadh. In the year following her tour, the number of women receiving breast cancer screenings at that Center increased almost five-fold, from an average of six patients a day to more than 25. In 2007, Mrs. Bush announced a new Partnership for Breast Cancer Awareness and Research of the Americas. Mrs. Bush attended events for this Partnership in Mexico and Panama.

In 2003, the National Heart, Lung, and Blood Institute of the National Institutes of Health invited Mrs. Bush to be the ambassador for their Heart Truth Campaign – a national initiative to raise awareness of heart disease in women. As part of this effort, Mrs. Bush gave speeches and interviews across the country to teach women about the risks of heart disease, the symptoms of a heart attack, and the keys to a heart-healthy lifestyle. The Heart Truth Campaign helped contribute to positive results: in 2003, one in three deaths among women was due to heart disease, but data from 2005 – the most recent year for which data is available – showed the number dropped to one in four deaths.

Mrs. Bush was also an ambassador for the President's health initiatives around the world – including the President's Emergency Plan for AIDS Relief and the President's Malaria Initiative (PMI). She visited twelve of the program's fifteen focus countries and ten of the fifteen countries the PMI has targeted with lifesaving services. In 2006, Mrs. Bush joined the President as co-host of the White House Summit on Malaria, which brought together experts from around the world to build a united front against this preventable disease. During the summit, President Bush announced the designation of eight additional countries as PMI target countries and expanded the "Volunteers for Prosperity" program to benefit organizations involved in the PMI.

Burma

Mrs. Bush has been an advocate and leading Administration voice for the cause of human rights in Burma. During the "Saffron Revolution" of 2007, Mrs. Bush criticized the atrocities committed by Burma's regime, and her efforts were acknowledged by UN Secretary-General Ban Ki-moon. After the devastation of Cyclone Nargis, which struck Burma in May 2008, Mrs. Bush held a press conference in the White House Press Briefing Room, where she called on the junta to allow unhindered access to international aid and to implement the good government they promised to their people. Three months later, Mrs. Bush traveled to the border between Burma and Thailand to see the plight of Burmese refugees firsthand. She toured the Mae La camp, the largest of nine refugee camps along the western Thailand border. She also visited the Mae Tao clinic, where refugees receive free medical treatment.

Natural, Cultural, and Historic Preservation

As a professional librarian, one of Mrs. Bush's top priorities was the National Book Festival. This project was inspired by her success with the Texas Book Festival, which was launched in 1995 and continues today. The first National Book Festival was held in partnership with the Library of Congress on September 8, 2001. It attracted approximately 30,000 readers to the National Mall. Seven years later, the Eighth

Annual National Book Festival attracted more than 70 authors and a crowd of more than 120,000. Participants took part in events ranging from storytelling by children's book authors to book signings by popular fiction writers.

Mrs. Bush continued to promote America's culture and heritage as Honorary Chair of the President's Committee on Arts and the Humanities. She visited museums and schools across the country, highlighting cultural initiatives like the National Endowment for the Humanities' Picturing America program and the National Endowment for the Arts' Big Read initiative. At the White House, Mrs. Bush honored winners of the National Medals for Museum and Library Services and the Coming Up Taller Awards. Mrs. Bush also joined the President for annual presentations of the National Medals of Arts and National Humanities Medals. In 2006, Mrs. Bush launched the Administration's Global Cultural Initiative, which encourages our Federal cultural agencies to implement art exchange programs as part of the U.S. diplomatic effort.

Mrs. Bush served as the honorary chair for Save America's Treasures, a public-private partnership that helps preserve individual landmarks and artifacts, and the Preserve America initiative, which was established by President Bush in 2003 to encourage communities across the Nation to improve access to local historic landmarks and cultural treasures. Mrs. Bush designated more than 700 Preserve America Communities in all fifty States and one U.S. territory, and joined the President in presenting 20 Preserve America Presidential Awards. Mrs. Bush also served as Honorary Chair of the National Park Foundation, and swore in hundreds of children to the National Park Service's Junior Ranger Program. In 2007, she announced another National Park Foundation program for youth, First Bloom, which brings city children to their nearest parks – and the ethic of conservation to America's backyards.

Lady Bird Johnson once said: "The Constitution of the United States does not mention the First Lady. She is elected by one man only. The statute books assign her no duties; and yet, when she gets the job, a podium is there if she cares to use it." Mrs. Bush used her podium to promote issues ranging from education to human rights. She was an effective ambassador for the President and a gracious representative of the American people in her travels across the country and the world.

★

THE FINAL YEAR

The President's final year in office was one of his most challenging and most productive. The President set a bold agenda on foreign and domestic policy and accomplished much of what he set out to do.

As the economy slowed at the start of the year, the President worked with Congress to pass an economic stimulus package. He secured Congressional approval for legislation to reauthorize and expand the President's Emergency Plan for AIDS Relief. He led efforts within the Group of Eight nations to ensure that going forward those countries are held accountable for commitments to provide assistance to developing countries. He secured passage of a new foreign terrorist surveillance law and Congressional approval for legislation to fund our troops – without conditions or artificial timetables for withdrawal in Iraq. He secured funding for the Merida Initiative, a partnership with Mexico and nations in Central America to crack down on violent drug trafficking gangs. He secured Congressional approval for an historic civil nuclear agreement with India that cemented the new relationship his Administration forged between the United States and India. He successfully pressed Congress to lift the ban on offshore oil exploration on the Outer Continental Shelf, expand access to oil shale, and approve tax credits to spur the development of alternative sources of energy like wind, solar, and nuclear power.

As the financial crisis unfolded in the fall, the President worked with Congressional leaders to pass a financial rescue package that helped prevent the collapse of the American financial system. And in December 2008, the President signed two historic agreements with the democratic government of Iraq that put America's engagement in Iraq on a strong and steady course and will help bring American troops home under a policy of "return on success."

This would be an outstanding list of accomplishments for any Administration in its first year – let alone its eighth year. Until his final moments in office, President Bush provided strong leadership for our Nation. And his achievements over eight years in the White House will stand the test of time. Guided by the President's leadership, America faced great challenges – and met them with determination. President Bush delivered on the promises he made for the American people. He rebuilt and transformed our Armed Forces. He reformed education, reduced taxes, and strengthened America's faith-based and community groups. He stood with veterans, expanded free trade, funded new energy technologies to reduce our dependence on foreign oil, improved our environment, and took on the challenge of climate change. He worked to reform our health care system, foster a culture of life, and appoint judges who respect our Constitution and laws, and do not legislate from the bench. He provided a way forward on challenges such as immigration and Social Security reform. And he protected America and spread freedom abroad.

On the steps of the United States Capitol eight years ago, President Bush quoted a letter that the Virginia statesman John Page wrote to Thomas Jefferson: "We know the race is not to the swift, nor the battle to the strong. Do you not think an angel rides in the whirlwind and directs this storm?" When President Bush spoke those words, neither he nor his listeners imagined the storms that were to come. Even those who disagree with the difficult decisions he made would agree that he was willing to make the difficult decisions. And he made them based on principle, and always in what he believed to be the best interests of our country.

LaVergne, TN USA
14 March 2010
175904LV00004BA/79/P